Application of Color to Reduce Complexity in Air Traffic Control

Tanya Yuditsky, Ph.D., ACB-220
Randy L. Sollenberger, Ph.D., ACB-220
Pamela S. Della Rocco, Ph.D., ACB-220
Ferne Friedman-Berg, Titan Systems
Carol A. Manning, Ph.D., AAM-510

DOT/FAA/CT-TN03/01

November 2002

Document is available to the public
through the National Technical Information
Service, Springfield, Virginia 22161

U.S. Department of Transportation
Federal Aviation Administration

William J. Hughes Technical Center
Atlantic City International Airport, NJ 08405

NOTICE

This document is disseminated under the sponsorship of the
U.S. Department of Transportation in the interest of information
exchange. The United States Government assumes no liability
for the contents or use thereof.

The United States Government does not endorse products or
manufacturers. Trade or manufacturer's names appear herein
solely because they are considered essential to the objective of
this report. This document does not constitute FAA
certification policy.

1. Report No. DOT/FAA/CT-TN03/01	2. Government Accession No.	3. Recipient's Catalog No.
4. Title and Subtitle Application of Color to Reduce Complexity in Air Traffic Control		5. Report Date November 2002
		6. Performing Organization Code ACB-220
7. Author(s) Tanya Yuditsky, Ph.D., Randy L. Sollenberger, Ph.D., and Pamela S. Della Rocco, Ph.D., ACB-220; Ferne Friedman-Berg, Titan Systems; and Carol A. Manning, Ph.D., AAM-510		8. Performing Organization Report No. DOT/FAA/CT-TN03/01
9. Performing Organization Name and Address Federal Aviation Administration William J. Hughes Technical Center Atlantic City International Airport, NJ 08405		10. Work Unit No. (TRAIS)
		11. Contract or Grant No.
12. Sponsoring Agency Name and Address Federal Aviation Administration Human Factors Division 800 Independence Ave., S.W. Washington, DC 20591		13. Type of Report and Period Covered Technical Note
		14. Sponsoring Agency Code AAR-100
15. Supplementary Notes		

16. Abstract

The United States Air Traffic Control (ATC) system is designed to provide for the safe and efficient flow of air traffic from origin to destination. The Federal Aviation Administration predicts that traffic levels will continue increasing over the foreseeable future. It is important to identify and reduce the factors that increase ATC complexity because of the potential consequences of errors. This research examined the application of specific information coding techniques to ATC displays as a method of reducing complexity in the en route environment. It tested color coding of (a) aircraft destination airport, (b) overflights, and (c) Special Use Airspace. Eight Certified Professional Controllers participated in the high fidelity, human-in-the-loop simulation. Results indicated that these specific enhancements may improve controller performance and efficiency. However, when we presented all of the enhancements simultaneously, we did not find the beneficial effects that occurred when we tested the enhancements individually. Further research is needed to systematically investigate the application of color to radar displays in the dynamic Air Traffic environment.

17. Key Words Air Traffic Control Color Displays Simulation Complexity	18. Distribution Statement This report is approved for public release and is on file at the William J. Hughes Technical Center, Aviation Security Research and Development Library, Atlantic City International Airport, New Jersey 08405. This document is available to the public through the National Technical Information Service, Springfield, Virginia, 22161.

19. Security Classif. (of this report) Unclassified	20. Security Classif. (of this page) Unclassified	21. No. of Pages 54	22. Price

Form DOT F 1700.7 (8-72)   **Reproduction of completed page authorized**

Table of Contents

Appendices

A - Informed Consent Form

B - Controller Background Questionnaire

C - Procedures for Measuring the CIE Chromaticity Coordinates of the Enhancement Colors

D - Over-The-Shoulder Observer Questionnaire

E - Observer Post-Scenario Questionnaire

F - Participant Post-Scenario Questionnaire

G - Participant Exit Questionnaire

H - Means (and Standard Deviations) by Scenario Type for all Aircraft

I - Means (and Standard Deviations) by Scenario Type for Enhanced Aircraft

List of Illustrations

Executive Summary

The United States Air Traffic Control (ATC) system provides for the safe and efficient flow of air traffic from origin to destination. The system is extremely complex and has many components. The Federal Aviation Administration predicts that traffic levels will increase over the foreseeable future. These projected increases will promote higher traffic density and pose substantial demands on the system and controller capacities. Mogford, Guttman, Morrow, and Kopardekar (1995) and Stein (1985) associated increasing levels of complexity with higher Air Traffic Control Specialist (ATCS) workload and, consequently, more operational errors. Mogford et al. defined ATC complexity as a construct composed of a number of dimensions or factors such as airspace structure, amount of climbing or descending traffic, the mix of aircraft types and flight rules, and presence of Special Use Airspace (SUA).

A recent study by Ahlstrom, Rubinstein, Siegel, Mogford, and Manning (2001) investigated how display enhancements can be used to present important information more directly to the controller, thereby reducing complexity. With help from ATCSs, the researchers developed four display solutions to the complexity-inducing effects of SUA, transitioning aircraft, weather, and reliability of radar/radio coverage. The current study investigated the effectiveness of the SUA and transitioning aircraft enhancements in a human-in-the-loop simulation. Specifically, this study investigated how the coding of overflights, aircraft destination airport, and active SUA affect controller performance, controller workload, and sector efficiency. We hypothesized that the automated visual cues depicting restricted airspace and identifying destination airport and overflights would reduce memory demands, reduce cognitive workload, and increase airspace efficiency.

Results indicated that there were significant effects on controller performance with each enhancement tested. Controllers issued fewer altitude clearances overall with the use of the overflight enhancement suggesting more efficient traffic flow. With the destination airport enhancement, we also found that controllers issued fewer altitude clearances for the arrival aircraft. Though the SUA enhancement did not affect any of the objective measures, our Operational Supervisor Observers rated the controllers as more effective at complying with the SUA restrictions and better able to handle heavy or unusual traffic with the SUA enhancement. When we presented all of the enhancements simultaneously, we did not find the beneficial effects that occurred when the enhancements were tested individually.

This was an exploratory study that looked at a small number of enhancement options. There are many more enhancements and many alternative coding techniques beyond what we explored. Further research is needed to address the questions of which enhancements are most beneficial and what is the most effective implementation. Until there is clearer guidance on these complex issues, we recommend that system designers exercise caution when developing future enhancements or Air Traffic tools that add color to the radar display.

1. Introduction

The United States Air Traffic Control (ATC) system provides for the safe and efficient flow of air traffic from origin to destination. The system is extremely complex and has many components. A typical commercial flight begins with preflight planning and data entry into the National Airspace System (NAS) database, taxi on the airport surface, departure from the airport of origin, and transition to desired altitudes. The aircraft then flies through the en route environment across multiple regional centers, each with multiple sectors. When the aircraft nears its destination, it reverses the process by descending, landing, taxiing, and finally delivering passengers to the gate. For each flight, multiple Air Traffic Control Specialists (ATCSs), monitor and direct the aircraft's progress to ensure its safety and to provide maximum efficiency.

This research examined the application of information coding enhancements in specific contexts as methods of reducing ATC complexity. Ahlstrom, Rubinstein, Siegel, Mogford, and Manning (2001) developed these enhancements through a series of prototyping and evaluation activities. The current study investigated the effectiveness of the enhancements in a human-in-the-loop simulation. Research psychologists from the NAS Human Factors Group (ACB-220) and from the Civil Aerospace Medical Institute (CAMI) conducted the simulations in the Research Development and Human Factors Laboratory (RDHFL) at the Federal Aviation Administration (FAA) William J. Hughes Technical Center (WJHTC). CAMI and the office of the Chief Scientific and Technical Advisor for Human Factors (AAR-100) sponsored the research.

The FAA predicts that traffic levels will continue increasing over the foreseeable future. These projected increases will promote higher traffic density and pose substantial demands on both system and controller capacities (Wickens, Mavor, & McGee, 1997; Wickens, Mavor, Parasuraman, & McGee, 1998). Increasing levels of ATC complexity have been associated with higher controller workload and, consequently, more operational errors (Mogford, Guttman, Morrow, & Kopardekar, 1995; Stein, 1985). Because of the potential consequences of errors, it is important to identify and reduce the factors that increase the complexity of ATC operations. This is particularly true in the en route environment, which encompasses the majority of the flight duration, provides the greatest flexibility for maneuvering, and may have the largest volume of high velocity aircraft operating on multiple routes at varying altitudes.

1.1 Background

To ensure safe separation of aircraft in the NAS, common ATC operations in the Air Route Traffic Control Centers (ARTCCs) include functions such as spacing and sequencing aircraft, transitioning aircraft to different altitudes, and rerouting aircraft around weather and restricted or Special Use Airspace (SUA). Within a sector of airspace, a controller monitors a radar display of the air traffic and exchanges information and issues clearances via voice radio. The controller may also interact with a radar associate and an assistant controller working in the sector, at adjacent sectors or ARTCCs, with the traffic management unit, and with the area supervisor.

The primary equipment the sector controller uses to perform these functions is a radar display, the Display System Replacement (DSR). The radar display includes maps depicting sector boundaries, routes, navigational aids, SUA, aircraft target symbols with associated data blocks containing important flight information, tabular lists, and weather depictions. A 20-in. square, color monitor with a Situation Display View, Display Controls (DC) and Status View, and a Computer Readout Device (CRD) View displays this information. Controllers can manage the information displayed and adjust display characteristics such as brightness through the DC View.

To input messages, controllers use the CRD, a keyboard, and a three-button trackball. The DSR color monitors, installed between 1998-2000, were the first color radar displays used at the 20 en route ARTCCs. At the time of this study, color coding was not used on the DSR display.

1.1.1 Complexity in ATC Operations

Several studies have examined factors associated with ATC complexity (Buckley, DeBaryshe, Hitchner, & Kohn, 1983; Mogford et al., 1995; Mogford, Murphy, Roske-Hofstrand, Yastrop, & Guttman, 1994). Mogford et al. defined ATC complexity as a construct composed of a number of complexity dimensions or factors. Such factors include airspace structure, number of intersecting airways, amount of climbing or descending traffic, mix of aircraft types and flight rules (i.e., instrument vs. visual flight rules), and presence of SUA and military traffic. The factors identified included the physical aspects of the sector (sector complexity) and the related movement and characteristics of the air traffic (traffic complexity) occupying the airspace. Mogford et al. observed that complexity generates controller workload. However, the workload can be mediated by the quality of the information display.

1.1.2 Information Coding Techniques

Techniques such as text coding (e.g., bold text), color coding, and flash coding can organize a display or call the user's attention to important information. The techniques vary in how many levels of each can be used effectively and in their attention-getting qualities (Ahlstrom & Longo, 2001). Therefore, some information coding techniques may be better than others in producing a desired effect. Likewise, inappropriate application of a coding technique may produce undesired effects. Flashing, for example, is a very strong attention-getting quality that should be used sparingly for situations where there is an urgent need for the user's attention. In today's ATC displays, flash coding is used to draw the controller's attention to situations where immediate user action is required. The Standard Terminal Automation Replacement System (STARS) and the DSR use flash coding to alert the controller of potential conflicts, aircraft that are in handoff status, and aircraft that are being pointed out by other controllers.

Several studies have evaluated the effects of modifications or enhancements to the ATC display. The coding technique investigated in many of these studies is the use of color. In operational reviews, controllers examined the use of color, dialogue design, and mouse data entry with the European Operational Display and Input Development (ODID) IV system (Graham, Young, Pichancourt, Marsden, & Irkitz, 1994; Krois & Marsden, 1997; Skiles, Graham, Marsden, & Krois, 1997). ODID IV used four colors (gray, pink, white, and mustard) to indicate different states of control of an aircraft. For example, gray indicated that an aircraft was not under the control of the ATCS. Pink indicated that an aircraft would be entering the controller's sector within 10 minutes. White indicated the aircraft was on frequency and that the ATCS had control. Mustard indicated that control had been handed off to another ATCS, but the aircraft was still within the sector. It used red and yellow as warning colors. Because this was an operational review, the authors made no objective or systematic measures of the effects of the enhancements or the use of color. However, controller comments supported the use of color as a display enhancement. The operational review of the other display enhancements showed that the dialogue design and mouse operations simplified information retrieval and data entry.

Ahlstrom, Rubinstein, et al. (2001) investigated how display enhancements can be used to present important information more directly to the controller, thereby reducing complexity. With help from ATCSs, the authors developed four display solutions to the complexity-inducing effects of SUA, transitioning aircraft, weather, and reliability of radar/radio coverage. All of these display enhancements used color to make important information readily available to the controller. The SUA enhancement used a color in-fill to indicate when the airspace was active and, in addition, presented text information on the times and altitudes of the activation. For transitioning aircraft, Ahlstrom, Rubinstein, et al. used color coding to identify overflights and to distinguish between different destination airports. The weather enhancement used color to present six levels of precipitation. In addition to the graphical representation, the display also presented text-based weather information (e.g., thunderstorms and turbulence). The radar/radio coverage enhancement used a color graphic on the sector map to represent a NAVAID outage. A system message window also presented specific text-based information on the outage.

A user evaluation of these display enhancements showed that en route controllers predicted a substantial reduction in job complexity with the use of the enhancements. The controllers reported that the amount of time that attention is diverted away from the radar screen is a major source of complexity. They identified the enhancements for transitioning aircraft and active SUA as potentially useful for maintaining attention on the radarscope because these enhancements reduce the need for checking flight strips and the information board. Controllers also identified the addition of memory aids for important information as a crucial complexity-reducing factor because it would attenuate memory failures and reduce cognitive workload. Each of the enhancements should reduce memory demands - some by providing information on the display that is currently not displayed, others by facilitating recognition of aircraft that match a certain criteria (e.g., arrivals at a particular airport). Because these display concepts could serve as important tools in the reduction of ATC complexity, it was important to formally evaluate their efficacy in operational systems. The present study evaluated the SUA and transitioning aircraft enhancements in the en route environment. Each of these enhancements uses color to highlight existing information on the display.

1.1.3 The Use of Color as a Display Enhancement

Some researchers have argued that color and differences in color are processed automatically (Triesman, 1986; Triesman & Gelade, 1980). Triesman and her colleagues proposed a theory of attention where basic visual features, such as color, are processed preattentively and in parallel across the visual field. This makes color an effective visual code that is quickly and easily noticed and provides additional information without increasing the demand on processing resources.

Many studies have examined the effects of color on target identification and search. Reviews of the literature (Christ, 1975; Cook, 1974) found that color-coding aids target identification and visual search. Subjects were faster and more accurate at identifying targets that were of a particular color than identifying targets that were of a particular shape, size, or brightness. The only feature that they found to be superior to color was alphanumeric symbols. The findings were similar in studies that used color as a redundant variable with size and/or brightness. When researchers asked subjects to locate or count targets that contain a specific feature, their search was faster when locating the target based on color than when based on size, brightness, shape, or alphanumeric symbol.

In addition, spatially separated targets can be perceptually grouped based on their color (Wickens & Hollands, 2000) following the Gestalt principles of perceptual grouping. This may be an especially useful feature when applied to the ATC environment where controllers have to integrate information about spatially separated aircraft. For instance, arrival aircraft for a particular airport may be approaching from different directions. The controller has to be aware of all of them in order to effectively sequence and space them for final approach. Color may be an especially effective cue for this task.

Reynolds (1994) used color to differentially emphasize information on the ATC display by applying more conspicuous colors to information that was more important to the controller. Though these display concepts were not formally tested, Reynolds anticipated the benefits to the controller to include a reduction in information processing of visually presented information and the capability to present additional, useful information on the display without increasing display complexity. Remington, Johnston, and Ruthruff (2000) color coded aircraft altitudes on the ATC display. They found that controllers were able to identify traffic conflicts more quickly when color coding was applied. Their explanation of the effect was that the color coding eliminated the need to fixate and attend to the altitude field in the aircraft data block. The controllers were able to determine whether two aircraft were of the same color and at the same altitude without focused spatial attention.

Color may be an appealing and effective display enhancement, but there are characteristics of the human visual system and of the displays that must be taken into consideration when applying color coding (Cardosi & Hannon, 1999). Guidelines have been established with respect to the use of color in computer displays (Mayhew, 1992), as well as specifically with ATC displays (Cardosi & Hannon; Reynolds, 1994). Many of the recommendations overlap. Mayhew recommends using color 1) sparingly (limited to eight distinct colors four are preferred), 2) to draw attention, communicate organization, indicate status, and establish relationships, 3) to support search tasks, 4) for consistent purpose and meaning, and 5) consistently with the cultural norms. Cardosi and Hannon recommend that the number of colors assigned for different purposes be limited to six. Both sets of guidelines recommend using redundant cues with color, particularly for critical information (Cardosi & Hannon; Mayhew). Other recommendations include avoiding the use of pure blue for text, small symbols, or background and sparing use of bright, highly saturated colors. It is also important to note that color sensitivity changes under different lighting conditions and with the capabilities of specific monitors.

In addition to identifying guidelines for the use of color, Cardosi and Hannon (1999) conducted three experiments using the Sony DDM-2801C (20 x 20) monitors, the same monitors as those used in DSR, to examine their color producing characteristics. In the series of studies, they examined variability across five different monitors, identified an "ideal" color set based on human visual system characteristics and the color production capabilities of the monitors, and assessed controller preferred colors. The results were several recommendations for ATC displays: 1) use a dark background, 2) green is a good color for data blocks on a dark background, 3) data blocks should be presented at medium intensity, 4) maintenance procedures are needed to ensure that monitors remain calibrated to sustain reliable colors, and 5) foreground and background must be considered together when selecting colors. They produced a derived color set for use with the displays. The color set included red, green, blue, white, yellow, magenta, and cyan. In their testing, cyan was the only color that was not discriminated at least 99% of the time with a black background. They noted that cyan was likely to be confused with white by people with the most common form of color deficiency and recommended that cyan not be used to code critical information.

Cardosi and Hannon (1999) warn that use of color may be so effective in categorizing aircraft that the controller may be less likely to notice a potential conflict between aircraft with different color codes. Studies have shown that people have difficulty integrating information across elements of a display that are of different colors as compared to elements that are of the same color (Wickens & Andre, 1990). Christ (1975) reported that the addition of color to an achromatic display interfered with the subjects' ability to identify or search for target features other than color (e.g., size or shape). The effects on identification were independent of whether the color was relevant or irrelevant. Search, however, seemed to only be affected when color was an irrelevant cue. The effects on search performance may be due to a change in the subjects' visual scanning patterns. Display factors such as color, brightness, or flashing have been found to affect the allocation of visual attention during a visual scan (Wickens & Hollands, 2000). This is a particularly important problem for ATC where visual scanning is critical in maintaining situational awareness. Disruptions to a controller's scan may lead to missed or delayed detection of a developing conflict (Stein, 1992) or increased focus on a particular area of the radar display (i.e., tunnel vision) (D'Arcy & Della Rocco, 2001).

1.2 Purpose and Hypotheses

The purpose of this study was to investigate how display enhancements depicting overflights, aircraft destination airport, and active SUA affect controller performance, controller workload, and sector efficiency. The development and testing of the display enhancements described in this report are a direct extension and operational evaluation of the concepts developed in the Ahlstrom, Rubinstein et al. (2001) study. Based on the findings in the color literature and the evaluation of the enhancements reported by Ahlstrom, Rubinstein et al., we hypothesized that the automated visual cues depicting restricted airspace and identifying transitioning aircraft will reduce memory demands, reduce cognitive workload, and increase controller efficiency. We expect that making this useful information more readily available to controllers will reduce ATC complexity and improve controller performance.

2. Method

We conducted a high fidelity, human-in-the-loop simulation. Controllers worked a simulated operational position and performed normal ATC functions. Two Supervisory ATCSs from the field functioned as members of the research team. They designed scenarios, developed the airspace procedures, and served as Operational Supervisor Observers during the simulation. They were recruited from level 11 and 12 ARTCCs.

2.1 Participants

Eight, en route, non-supervisory Certified Professional Controllers (CPCs) participated in the study. We solicited participants nationwide from levels 11 and 12 ARTCCs. Each participant was current and held a current ATC medical certificate. This ensured that the participants had normal or corrected-to-normal vision, normal health, and normal hearing. The controllers completed Informed Consent Forms (see Appendix A) prior to participating in the study.

Each controller completed a Background Questionnaire (see Appendix B). Controllers ranged in age from 31 to 43 years ($M = 38.6$, $SD = 4.0$) with 9 to 18 years of experience in ATC ($M = 13.4$, $SD = 3.1$). All of the participants had experience working a transition sector. Only one of the participants worked in an area where there was no SUA. The others worked in areas where SUA became active on a daily basis.

We tested controllers' color vision by using the Pseudo-Isochromatic Ishihara Plate Test (Ishihara, 1997). Controllers viewed a series of colored numbers against different colored backgrounds. The plates contain figures and backgrounds whose colors (hues) belong to sets confused by people with color deficiencies. Normal observers will see one series of numbers, whereas color deficient observers will either see no number or a different number than normals. All of the participants responded correctly to all of the plates.

2.2 Display Enhancements

The enhancements that we tested in this study were color coding of 1) overflights, 2) aircraft destination airport, and 3) SUA. We implemented coding of overflights and aircraft destination airport by applying color to a specific portion of the aircraft data block. The data block consists of three lines of information about the aircraft, including its call sign, altitude, and speed. Arrival aircraft often include an airport identifier for their destination airport.

For the overflight enhancement, we colored the altitude field in the second line of the data block green (Figure 1A). We defined overflights as level flying aircraft that were not departures from or arrivals to the airports that are directly fed by the sector.

For the destination airport enhancement, we colored the airport identifier in the third line of the data block. We used two colors, magenta (Figure 1B) and cyan (Figure 1C), to represent two different destinations. The display enhancement for active SUA consisted of a red outline of active areas on the radar display. Five minutes prior to activation, a system message window displayed text-based information specifying the affected area, altitudes, and activation times.

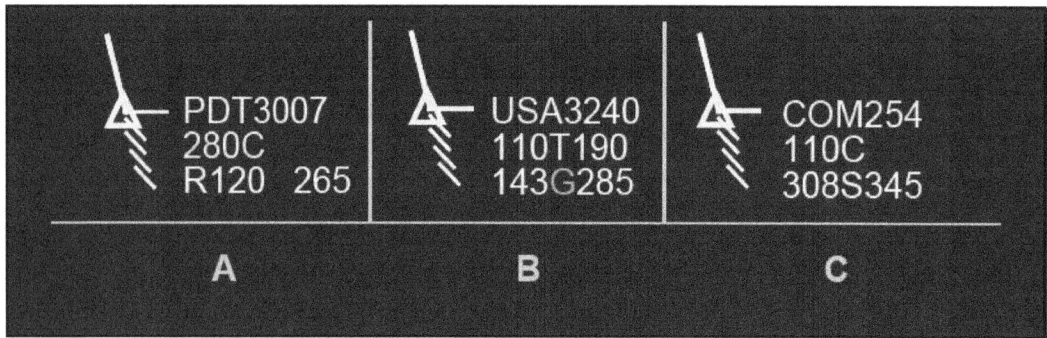

Figure 1. An illustration of the (a) overflight and (b,c) destination airport enhancements

An important consideration in implementing these enhancements was selecting the colors to use. The focus of this study was on testing the concept of using color to make information more readily available to the controller, not on determining which colors were best suited for the enhancements. In making our selection, we applied guidelines on the use of color (Cardosi & Hannon, 1999; Mayhew, 1992). We selected colors that were easily distinguished from those already present in the DSR display, did not interfere with the readability of data blocks, and did not relay inappropriate meaning (e.g., using the color green to indicate an active SUA may lead to confusion over whether the airspace is available).

The colors we used, magenta, cyan, green, and red, are among the set of maximally discriminable colors on a cathode ray tube display (Cardosi & Hannon, 1999). We used cyan even though Cardosi and Hannon reported that people with the most common color deficiency might confuse it with white. We eliminated the potential of confusing cyan with white by testing

6

our participants' color vision and not using white for any of the enhancements. Therefore, as long as the controllers were able to differentiate the cyan objects from the rest of the data block (displayed in an orange/yellow color), they should not have had any difficulty in discriminating the cyan coding. Table 1 presents the 1931 CIE chromaticity coordinates and luminance values for the colors. We describe the procedures for measuring these values in Appendix C.

Table 1. Enhancement Colors' Mean CIE Chromaticity Coordinates and Luminance

Color	x	y	L[a]
Cyan	.197	.248	8.90
Magenta	.275	.148	4.87
Green	.288	.561	14.04
Red	.598	.334	0.77

[a] candelas per square meter

2.3 Airspace and Scenarios

For this experiment, the research team developed a generic airspace sector (See Figure 2) that contained multiple departure and arrival routes, several prominent fixes and intersections, and six SUA areas (R1001-R1006). This low altitude (surface to 24,000 ft.), en route, transition sector fed traffic to and from a major airport, Genera (GEN), as well as three satellite airports, Uptown (UPT), Downtown (DWN), and Midtown (MID). We identified aircraft arriving at GEN with a "G" identifier, and those arriving at any of the satellite airports with an "S" identifier. Creating a generic airspace allowed us to ensure that all controllers had equal familiarity with the sector (Guttman & Stein, 1997; Guttman, Stein, & Gromelski, 1995). It also allowed us to design an airspace that met the needs of the experiment.

The Ahlstrom, Rubinstein et al. (2001) study found that controllers rated the display enhancements for transitioning aircraft as more or less useful depending on the traffic flow that was common to their sector. For this reason, the combination of scenario and enhancement was a critical component of the present study. The scenarios included traffic conditions and/or restrictions that should have maximized the usefulness of the display enhancements being evaluated. For example, we intended the display enhancement that color coded overflights to highlight the aircraft that were flying level in a sector that was primarily made up of climbing and descending traffic. By using this display enhancement, we hoped to highlight the aircraft that added complexity to the normal traffic flow.

Using the same sector for all scenarios provided a standard traffic flow that was primarily arrivals and departures with some overflights. The differences were in the restrictions that were in effect and the enhancements that we used. We developed four enhancement conditions: three to test each of the three enhancements individually and one to test the combination of all enhancements. We describe the enhancement conditions in the sections that follow.

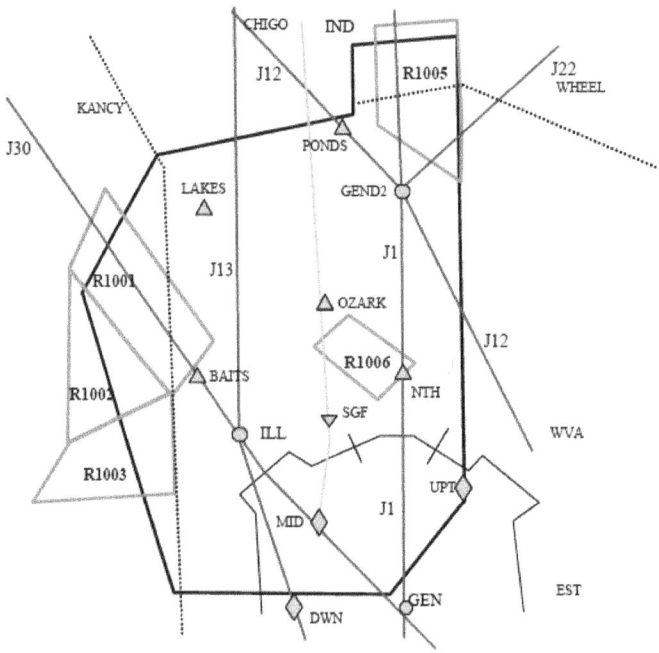

Figure 2. Genera sector map.

For each enhancement condition, we developed two comparable scenarios. Table 2 presents some of the traffic characteristics for the scenarios. Each scenario started with approximately 10 aircraft in the sector and lasted 45 minutes.

Table 2. Scenario Characteristics

Enhancement Condition	Scenario	Aircraft Count	Number of Arrivals	Number of Departures	Number of Overflights
En Route	*En Route 1*	76	37	13	26
	En Route 2	70	35	14	21
Arrival	*Arrival 1*	69	38	12	19
	Arrival 2	70	42	12	16
SUA	*SUA 1*	61	29	15	17
	SUA 2	65	34	15	16
All Enhancements	*All 1*	77	37	19	21
	All 2	77	37	20	20

2.3.1 En Route Scenarios and the Overflight Enhancement

We designed the En Route scenario to assess the effectiveness of highlighting overflights in a sector where traffic primarily consisted of arrivals and departures. Overflights add complexity to a transition sector because the controller must direct the level-flying overflight aircraft through the existing flows of climbing and descending aircraft. We expected the overflight enhancement to help the controller by highlighting aircraft that were different from the established traffic flow and required a different response. In the En Route scenario, we added several overflight aircraft to the standard traffic flow. In the experimental condition, we applied the overflight enhancement to all overflight aircraft. In the control condition, we presented the same traffic patterns without the use of display enhancements.

2.3.2 Arrival Scenarios and the Destination Airport Enhancement

The rules and restrictions governing the approaches to specific airports add complexity to a transition sector. Altitude restrictions over an arrival fix may vary depending on the type of aircraft. These restrictions require that the controller descend the aircraft to the appropriate altitude before it reaches the fix. Miles-in-Trail (MIT) restrictions impose spacing requirements on arrival flows. The controller must use various techniques to increase the spacing between aircraft that are headed to a particular airport.

In the Arrival scenario, we implemented two sets of altitude restrictions based on aircraft type, one for GEN and one for the satellite airports. For GEN arrivals, jets, turboprops, and props had to cross the arrival fixes at 14000, 12000, and 10000 ft, respectively. For satellite arrivals, the restrictions were 10000, 8000, and 6000 ft, respectively. We expected controllers to use the destination airport enhancement to distinguish between aircraft arriving at various airports and, based on that information, to quickly identify the restrictions that apply to that aircraft.

The Arrival scenario also imposed a 10-mile MIT spacing restriction for GEN over Illinois (ILL) arrival fix. The restriction took effect 10 minutes into the scenario and continued for the duration of the problems. Because the arrival traffic for all of the airports came in over the same arrival fixes, we expected the destination airport enhancement to help controllers quickly identify the aircraft that had to be spaced, thereby allowing them to be more effective in meeting the restriction. In the experimental condition, we color coded the airport identifiers. In the control condition, we presented the same traffic patterns without the use of display enhancements.

2.3.3 SUA Scenarios and the SUA Enhancement

We designed the SUA scenario to evaluate the effectiveness of highlighting active SUA. ATC complexity is increased when SUA becomes active because controllers must reroute traffic around the area. In order to do this effectively, they must keep in mind the activation times and plan accordingly. To maintain optimal efficiency, they must also remember when the SUA becomes available again so that they can return to normal, more direct routing. Complexity is increased further when different areas become active or available at different times.

The SUA scenario added activation of several SUA areas to the basic traffic flows through the sector. Areas R1001, R1002, R1003, and R1005 were active at 10 minutes into the scenario. At 25 minutes, areas R1001, R1002, and R1003 became available, and area R1006 became active. Areas R1005 and R1006 remained active until the end of the scenario. We expected activation of areas R1001 and R1006 to have a particularly large impact on ATC complexity because R1001 affects a main arrival route (J30), and R1006 affects the primary departure route from GEN (J1). In the experimental condition, a text box was presented on the radar display 5 minutes prior to activation specifying the name of the area, the affected altitudes, and activation times. The text box remained on the display until the area became available. While the SUA was active, it was colored red. In the control condition, the controllers received a 5-minute verbal warning prior to activation. Also, we wrote the name of the area, affected altitudes, and activation times on an information board. Color coding was not used to indicate SUA activity.

2.3.4 All Enhancements Scenario

We developed this scenario to investigate how the display of multiple enhancements affects complexity. The All Enhancements scenario presented a basic traffic flow with altitude restrictions over the arrival fixes and SUA R1006 active for 15 minutes during the problem. In the experimental condition, we used all of the enhancements. In the control condition, we presented the same traffic patterns without the use of display enhancements.

2.4 Simulation Setup

The appearance of colors can change based on the color of the background, the brightness of the display, and ambient light levels. To minimize these effects, background color, brightness, and ambient lighting remained constant throughout the study. The DC View controls the brightness levels for all of the display objects on the DSR display. In order to determine appropriate brightness levels for the displays, we collected brightness settings from operational displays in the field. We implemented the most commonly used DC View settings (Table 3) on the experimental displays.

Table 3. Experimental Display DSR Brightness Settings

Brightness Group	Brightness Value
Full data blocks	90
Target	90
History	64
Map1	54
Map2	46
Sector	70
Master	90
Background	20

DC View brightness settings range from 0 to 100. The DSR background color changes from bright blue to black as brightness decreases. The low level of brightness used in this study represented a very dark (almost black) background.

The controller workstation contained a Sony (20x20) monitor, a DSR keyboard, and three-button trackball. The Distributed Environment for Simulation, Rapid Engineering, and Experimentation (DESIREE) and the WJHTC Target Generation Facility (TGF) simulation engine displayed and drove the traffic scenarios, respectively. The NAS Simulation Group (ACB-480) of the WJHTC developed DESIREE. It is a simulator that emulates the display and functions of the DSR,

10

whereas the TGF provides aircraft position and flight characteristics. Together with the TGF, DESIREE provided the combined capability of conducting a high fidelity human-in-the-loop simulation and incorporating all of the enhancements into a DSR display.

We printed and time-ordered flight progress strips in strip bays prior to the start of each scenario. We located information boards for posting SUA information within each controller's view. We positioned the Air Traffic Workload Input Technique (ATWIT) response device, a liquid crystal display touch screen, within the controller's reach. We used low light cameras to record video and audio of each experimental run.

2.5 Measures

We used both objective and subjective measures during the simulation. In addition, we used two preliminary measures: one to assess the effectiveness of the enhancements in a non-operational setting and the other to evaluate how well the controllers learned our generic airspace.

2.5.1 Preliminary Measures

2.5.1.1 Display Enhancements Decision Task

As part of assessing the effectiveness of the enhancements, the controllers completed a Display Enhancements Decision Task. We designed this two-alternative, forced choice, decision task to compare decision response times to targets with and without enhancements.

We used two types of questions. One type asked which aircraft is going to a particular airport. The second asked which aircraft is at a particular altitude. We manipulated presentation type with three levels. In the Enhanced condition, we enhanced the correct answer. In the Incorrect Enhanced condition, we enhanced the distractor. In the No Enhancement (control) condition, we did not use enhancements. We included the Incorrect Enhanced condition to prevent the controllers from simply responding to the presence of color. We counterbalanced the presentation of the target on the left or right of the display across the presentation conditions.

We recorded the accuracy and response times for each trial. If the enhancements were effective in attention getting, we expected the participants to attend to the enhanced target first. Response times would then be fastest in the Enhanced condition where the correct answer was enhanced. In the Incorrect Enhanced condition, where the incorrect target was enhanced, the participants could evaluate the enhanced target and reject it more quickly. This behavior would lead to response times that were faster or comparable to response times when neither of the targets was enhanced. Alternatively, the color coding of the distractor may distract the participants. In that case, we would predict slower response times in the Incorrect Enhanced condition than in the control.

2.5.1.2 Map Test

To assess how well the controllers learned the generic airspace, we administered a Map Test. We tested the controllers' memories for key elements of the sector by asking them to fill in the missing names of three airports, four fixes, and five SUA areas. We did not warn the controllers that their memory would be tested because we wanted to get a measure of how much they remember based on the opening briefing and training scenarios rather than how much they can memorize.

11

2.5.2 Air Traffic Measures

We recorded six objective dependent variables in all conditions: 1) aircraft time in sector, 2) total distance flown, 3) number of operational errors, 4) number of altitude changes, 5) number of heading changes, and 6) number of speed changes. The number of operational errors is often used as a measure of air traffic safety. The other measures are objective indicators of controller efficiency. Reductions in the numbers of altitude or heading changes, for example, can be indicative of more efficient operations. If display enhancements were effective in reducing ATC complexity, we hypothesized that all of these measures would be reduced when using the enhancements.

Depending on the traffic conditions and the enhancements being used in a scenario, we recorded some additional measures. When a scenario involved activation of SUA, we recorded the number of operational deviations where aircraft entered the airspace while it was active. We also examined activity in the SUA just after it was released to evaluate whether the use of the enhancement improved the controllers' awareness of SUA availability. Without the enhancement, controllers may not realize that SUA activation had terminated and may continue rerouting aircraft around the area. We hypothesized that controllers would be more efficient in rerouting aircraft when using display enhancements. That is to say, they will have fewer airspace deviations and fewer unnecessary reroutes after activation when SUA activation is color coded.

When a scenario involved altitude or MIT restrictions, we recorded the proportion of aircraft that met the restrictions. We expected that display enhancements would help controllers identify aircraft that were subject to the restrictions more readily. This should result in more aircraft meeting the restrictions in the enhanced scenarios.

2.5.3 Push-To-Talk

We recorded the number and duration of controller-pilot communications. We expected these measures to covary with air traffic measures such as the number of heading and altitude changes. We anticipated finding decreases in these measures when using the enhancements.

2.5.4 Subjective Measures

We collected subjective ratings from Over-The-Shoulder Observer Questionnaires (Sollenberger, Stein, & Gromelski, 1996; Vardaman & Stein, 1998) (see Appendix D), Observer Post-Scenario Questionnaires (see Appendix E), and Participant Post-Scenario Questionnaires (see Appendix F) after each test run. These questionnaires addressed controller performance, the difficulty and realism of the scenarios, and the usefulness of the display enhancements. We also used the ATWIT (Stein, 1985; Stein, 1991) to collect workload ratings at 5-minute intervals throughout the scenarios. We used a final controller questionnaire (see Appendix G) to collect additional ratings on the overall effects of the enhancements.

2.6 Procedure

Controllers arrived at the RDHFL in pairs for a week of simulation testing and evaluation. We scheduled Monday and Friday for travel. Tuesday's schedule consisted of an introductory briefing, a color vision test, sector training, three 30-minute simulation practice scenarios, the map test, and the Display Enhancements Decision Task. Controllers completed an Informed Consent Form and a Background Questionnaire before participating in the study.

12

After completing all of the practice scenarios, participants completed the Map Test. We asked them to fill in the missing names on the map to the best of their ability.

We instructed the participants on the procedures for the Display Enhancements Decision Task. We asked them to respond to each question as quickly and as accurately as possible. To familiarize participants with the experimental procedure and the various conditions, we presented 18 practice trials, with 6 trials for each of the three presentation conditions, at the beginning of the experiment. We randomized the order of presentation. We started each trial by presenting a question on the display. Participants pressed a key when they finished reading the question. After a 500 ms blank display, we presented two targets, one of which was the correct answer to the question. Participants responded by pressing a key on the keyboard. They pressed the "/" key on the right side of the keyboard if the target on the right was the correct response. They pressed the "Z" key on the left side of the keyboard if the target on the left was the correct response. After the response, we cleared the display and displayed the response time for that trial for 2 seconds. This task took approximately 15 minutes to complete.

We presented the air traffic test scenarios over 2 days. At the beginning of each day of test runs, we provided the controllers with a brief refresher on sector characteristics and the use of display enhancements. During all scenarios, the controllers used standard ATC procedures, issued commands to simulation pilots, and coordinated with "ghost controllers" from adjacent sectors. Operational Supervisor Observers provided notification of SUA activation and conducted over-the-shoulder observations of the controllers. Each run began with a relief briefing from the Operational Supervisor describing the traffic that was in the sector. After each run, the Operational Supervisor Observers and the controllers completed Post-Scenario Questionnaires. After the last test scenario, the controllers and researchers discussed their experiences in the study. The controllers completed an Exit Questionnaire that asked them to rate the overall effects of the enhancements.

2.7 Experimental Design

We treated this study as four independent experiments. In each experiment (i.e., enhancement condition), we compared the effects of using a specific enhancement or combination of enhancements to a control condition (no enhancements).

For each enhancement condition, ATC subject matter experts created two similar scenarios to avoid potential learning effects from a controller experiencing the same scenario twice. Table 2 presented the traffic characteristics of these scenarios. Each controller experienced every scenario once. Half of the participants experienced the first scenario in the enhanced condition, and the other half experienced this scenario in the control condition. Because the factors of scenario and experimental condition were not completely crossed, we balanced the order of presentation to minimize the potential effects of differential difficulty between the scenarios. This resulted in a replicated Latin Square design (Table 4) for each enhancement condition.

We wanted to balance any learning effects across all of the experiments. We developed a total of eight scenarios for the four enhancement conditions as follows: En Route 1, En Route 2; Arrival 1, Arrival 2; SUA 1, SUA 2; All 1, and All 2. We also developed a moderate traffic level Arrival scenario (Arrival M), which was not included in the analysis.

Table 4. Latin Square Design for one Enhancement Condition

Row[a]	Participant	Scenario 1	Scenario 2
1	1	Enhanced	Control
2	2	Control	Enhanced
1	3	Enhanced	Control
2	4	Control	Enhanced
1	5	Enhanced	Control
2	6	Control	Enhanced
1	7	Enhanced	Control
2	8	Control	Enhanced

[a] the combination of scenario and experimental condition

To balance presentation order across all conditions, we combined all of the scenarios and developed the presentation order using a modified Latin Square. The modification was the condition that the SUA scenarios were always experienced on the last day of the study. The SUA scenarios were quite difficult because they included the activation and deactivation of several SUA areas and required reroutes of several traffic flows. This ordering ensured that the participants had as much experience with the airspace, its fixes, and jetways as possible before having to reroute aircraft around multiple active SUA. Table 5 presents the resulting order for each participant.

Table 5. Scenarios Presented to Each Participant

Participant	Run 1	Run 2	Run 3	Run 4	Run 5	Run 6	Run 7	Run 8	Run 9
1	ARR 1 Enh	ENR 1 Control	ARR M	ALL 1 Enh	ARR 2 Control	SUA 1 Enh	ENR 2 Enh	All 2 Control	SUA 2 Control
2	ALL 2 Enh	ARR 1 Control	ENR 1 Enh	ARR M	ALL 1 Control	SUA 2 Enh	ARR 2 Enh	ENR 2 Control	SUA 1 Control
3	ENR 2 Enh	ALL 2 Control	ARR 1 Enh	ENR 1 Control	ARR M	SUA 2 Control	ALL 1 Enh	ARR 2 Control	SUA 1 Enh
4	ARR 2 Enh	ENR 2 Control	ALL 2 Enh	ARR 1 Control	ENR 1 Enh	SUA 1 Control	ARR M	All 1 Control	SUA 2 Enh
5	ALL 1 Enh	ARR 2 Control	ENR 2 Enh	All 2 Control	ARR 1 Enh	SUA 1 Enh	ENR 1 Control	ARR M	SUA 2 Control
6	ARR M	ALL 1 Control	ARR 2 Enh	ENR 2 Control	ALL 2 Enh	SUA 2 Enh	ARR 1 Control	ENR 1 Enh	SUA 1 Control
7	ENR 1 Control	ARR M	ALL 1 Enh	ARR 2 Control	ENR 2 Enh	SUA 2 Control	All 2 Control	ARR 1 Enh	SUA 1 Enh
8	ARR 1 Control	ENR 1 Enh	ARR M	ALL 1 Control	ARR 2 Enh	SUA 1 Control	ENR 2 Control	ALL 2 Enh	SUA 2 Enh

14

Though the order of presentation combined all four experiments, the analysis treated each experiment independently. This presentation order for all of the scenarios maintained the replicated Latin Square for each enhancement condition that Table 4 described.

2.8 Analysis

We analyzed the results from the preliminary measures (the Display Enhancements Decision Task and the Map Test) separately. For the Display Enhancements Decision Task, which was a within subjects design, we used a two-way analysis of variance (ANOVA). We examined the effects of question type and presentation condition.

For the experimental results, we performed the analyses based on the replicated Latin Square design utilized in each of the four experiments. To test the effects of our enhancements, we analyzed each study using ANOVAs. We examined the simple main effects of a) experimental condition, b) scenario, c) row (of the Latin Square), and d) participant. Because these factors were not completely crossed in the design, we did not add interaction terms to our model. However, as pointed out by Myers and Well (1991), if there are interactions or non-additivity in the sampled population, the result is a possible decrease in power and a possible increase in Type 2 error rates.

3. Results

In the following sections we report the results of the preliminary measures followed by the experimental measures.

3.1 Display Enhancements Decision Task

We analyzed correct responses for six of the eight participants. Data for the two remaining participants were not used because the participants only experienced two of the three conditions. Overall accuracy in the training task was very high ($M = 95\%$, $SD = 4\%$).

Figure 3 presents the mean response times (RTs). For the Airport question, asking which aircraft was going to a particular airport, the mean RTs for the three presentation conditions were 723.2 ms ($SD = 295.1$) in the control (No Enhancement) condition, 561.6 ms ($SD = 167.8$) in the Enhanced, and 611.9 ms ($SD = 135.76$) in the Incorrect Enhanced condition.

For the Altitude question, asking which aircraft was at a particular altitude, the mean RTs for the three presentation conditions were 653.4 ms ($SD = 165.7$) in the control condition, 635.4 ms ($SD = 208.2$) in the Enhanced condition, and 696.6 ms ($SD = 247.7$) in the Incorrect Enhanced condition.

We used a 2x3 ANOVA to analyze the RTs for correct responses. The analysis revealed a significant interaction of question type and presentation condition [$F(2, 10) = 4.73$, $p < .01$]. Simple main effects for the Airport question revealed a significant main effect of presentation condition [$F(2, 10) = 8.94$, $p < .01$]. We analyzed differences between the three means using Tukey's HSD post hoc comparisons. All significant post hoc results are at the alpha = .05 level. The results indicated that responses were significantly faster in the Enhanced and the Incorrect Enhanced than the control condition. There was no reliable difference between RTs in the Enhanced and Incorrect Enhanced conditions. Simple main effects for the Altitude question indicated that the main effect of presentation condition was not significant.

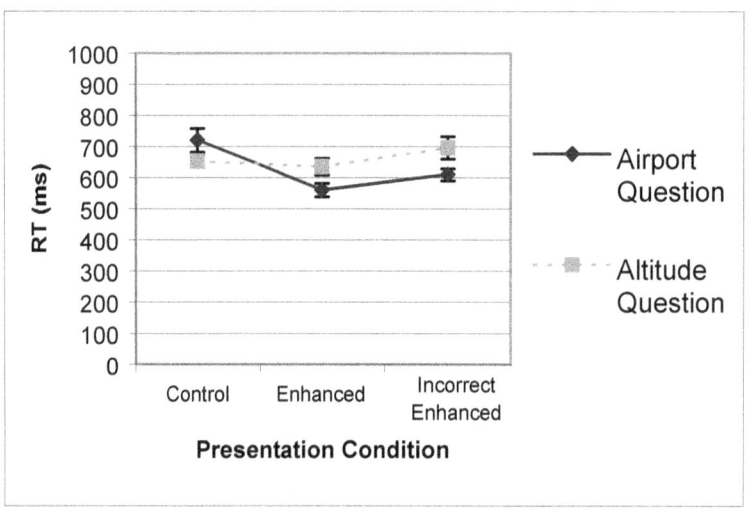

Figure 3. Mean RT (and standard error) for each question type by presentation condition.

3.2 Map Test

The Map Test contained 12 fill-in-the-blank questions. The mean percent correct was 76% (*SD* = 22%). The range of scores was between 100% and 42% correct. The participant who scored 42% was not an outlier in any of the other analyses.

3.3 Air Traffic Measures

We analyzed six dependent air traffic variables: 1) total aircraft time in sector (s), 2) total distance flown (nm), 3) number of operational errors, 4) number of altitude changes, 5) number of heading changes, and 6) number of speed changes. We compared the enhanced and control conditions for each measure for each enhancement condition. We excluded three cases from the analyses because the data files were incomplete: one from the En Route scenarios, one from the Arrival scenarios, and one from the SUA scenarios.

3.4 Air Traffic Measures – All Aircraft

These analyses included all aircraft in the scenarios. Appendix H presents the means and standard deviations for these measures.

In the En Route scenarios, the controllers made fewer altitude changes when using the overflight enhancement (*M* = 63.9, *SD* = 6.1) than in the control condition (*M* = 70.4, *SD* = 5.6), $F(1,5) = 10.56, p < .05$.

In the Arrival scenarios, the controllers issued fewer heading changes in the enhanced condition (*M* = 24.6, *SD* = 6.7) than in the control (*M* = 33.1, *SD* = 8.6), $F(1,5) = 16.87, p = .01$. There was also a significant effect of scenario for number of heading changes in the Arrival scenarios, with more heading changes made in the Arrival 1 scenario (*M* = 32.1, *SD* = 9.5) than Arrival 2 (*M* = 25.6, *SD* = 6.9), $F(1,5) = 8.28, p < .05$.

3.5 Air Traffic Measures – Enhanced Aircraft

We repeated the analysis of air traffic measures for the specific aircraft that had enhancements applied to their data blocks. Whereas the analysis of all aircraft provided an overall picture of the effects, this analysis looked specifically at the aircraft that were highlighted by the enhancements. In the En Route scenarios, we analyzed the overflights. In the Arrival scenarios, we analyzed the arrivals. In the All Enhancements scenarios, we analyzed both overflights and arrivals. We report the means and standard deviations for the enhanced aircraft in Appendix I.

Analyses of the enhanced aircraft in the Arrival scenarios revealed significant effects of experimental condition on the number of heading changes, $F(1,5) = 10.32, p < .05$, and the number of altitude changes, $F(1,5) = 22.22, p = .01$. Controllers made fewer heading and altitude changes in the enhanced condition ($M = 12.6, SD = 4.9$ for heading and $M = 42.7, SD = 2.4$ for altitude) than in the control ($M = 19.3, SD = 8.4$ and $M = 46.6, SD = 3.6$).

We also found several significant effects of scenario. In the En Route scenarios, there was a significant effect of scenario for total time flown. Total time flown was shorter in the En Route 1 scenario ($M = 23188.4, SD = 4459.5$) than En Route 2 ($M = 25428.4, SD = 3860.7$), $F(1,5) = 17.21, p = .01$. In the Arrival scenarios, there were more heading changes in Arrival 1 ($M = 20.0, SD = 8.1$) than Arrival 2 ($M = 11.9, SD = 4.0$), $F(1,5) = 17.29, p = .01$. In the All Enhancements scenarios, there were fewer altitude changes in All 1 ($M = 43.5, SD = 8.0$) than All 2 ($M = 46.9, SD = 6.6$), $F(1,6) = 10.17, p < .05$.

3.6 Air Traffic Measures – Compliance With Restrictions

We analyzed how effective controllers were at complying with the restrictions that were imposed in the scenarios. We hypothesized that the enhancements would help the controllers to meet the restrictions by highlighting relevant information on the display.

3.6.1 SUA Activation

We predicted that controllers would be better at avoiding active SUA and more effective at utilizing inactive SUA when they used the SUA enhancement. We expected the enhancement would act as a visual reminder of SUA status. This behavior would be reflected in lower frequency and duration of aircraft flying through SUA when the area is active and higher frequency and duration of aircraft flying through the area shortly after it becomes inactive. Resuming the use of the area promptly after deactivation indicates a return to more efficient routing of aircraft through the sector.

We present the number of aircraft that crossed the SUA during times when the areas were active (hot) and the total duration of flying times through the areas in Table 6.

Table 6. Number of Aircraft Entering the SUA and Total Flight Times During Active Periods

Enhancement Condition	Measure	Enhanced M (SD)	Control M (SD)
SUA	Number of aircraft	1.1 (1.4)	1.0 (0.8)
	Flight time (s)	48.7 (74.3)	34.7 (45.5)
All Enhancements	Number of aircraft	1.0 (1.4)	2.0 (3.2)
	Flight time (s)	52.4 (88.2)	156.8 (313.8)

17

We also present the number of aircraft that crossed the SUA and the total duration of flying times in the 5 minutes after deactivation, when the areas became inactive (cold) in Table 7. We compared the enhanced and control conditions for the SUA and All Enhancements scenarios. Because the frequency of violations was very low, we were unable to detect any differences in the absolute frequency or duration of use for the enhanced versus the control conditions. Many of the findings, however, showed the expected pattern of results.

We performed a binomial analysis to test whether any significant patterns exist in the predicted direction. For the SUA scenarios, only two of the four comparisons showed a difference in the predicted direction; frequency and duration of aircraft flying through inactive SUA increased in the enhanced condition. For the All Enhancements scenarios, however, four out of four comparisons showed differences in the predicted direction. This pattern approached significance ($p = .06$).

Table 7. Number of Aircraft Entering the SUA and Total Flight Times 5 Minutes After Deactivation

Enhancement Condition	Measure	Enhanced M (SD)	Control M (SD)
SUA	**Number of aircraft**	1.3 (0.5)	1.0 (0.0)
	Flight time (s)	170.1 (130.7)	108.7 (24.1)
All Enhancements	**Number of aircraft**	1.4 (0.9)	1.1 (1.3)
	Flight time (s)	89.9 (81.6)	61.1 (71.8)

3.6.2 Altitude Restrictions

We analyzed all arrival aircraft that flew over the arrival fixes (SGF and ILL) for the scenarios that used the destination airport enhancement (Arrival and All Enhancements). We compared each aircraft's altitude over the fix to the specified altitude for that aircraft type and its destination airport to see if it met the restriction. Overall, compliance with the restrictions was high ($M = 85\%$, $SD = 15\%$). We did not find any significant differences between the enhanced and control conditions.

3.6.3 MIT Restrictions

We analyzed the proportion of aircraft that met the 10-mile MIT restriction imposed on GEN arrivals in the Arrival scenarios. The effect of experimental condition was not statistically significant, but there was a reliable effect of scenario, $F(1, 5) = 22.40$, $p < .01$. Controllers were better at meeting the MIT restriction in traffic sample 1 ($M = 0.83$, $SD = 0.15$) than in traffic sample 2 ($M = 0.71$, $SD = 0.10$).

3.7 Push-To-Talk

There was a significant main effect of experimental condition on the duration of controller-pilot communications in the Arrival scenarios, $F(1, 6) = 10.59, p < .05$, with shorter communications occurring in the enhanced condition ($M = 722.75, SD = 112.80$) than in the control condition ($M = 768.88, SD = 109.06$).

3.8 ATWIT

Controllers rated workload using ATWIT ratings at 5-minute intervals throughout the scenarios. We analyzed mean ATWIT ratings for the entire 45-minute scenario run time. Table 8 presents the mean workload ratings for the enhanced and control conditions. We compared ratings between the enhanced and control conditions for each enhancement condition. We did not find any significant differences between the enhanced and control conditions. The enhancements did not reduce or increase perceived workload.

Table 8. Mean ATWIT Ratings (and Standard Deviations)

Enhancement Condition	Enhanced	Control
En Route	4.2 (1.5)	4.5 (1.8)
Arrival	4.5 (2.1)	4.5 (1.8)
SUA	5.2 (2.0)	4.7 (2.0)
All Enhancements	5.3 (2.1)	5.4 (2.1)

3.9 Observer Over-the-Shoulder Ratings

Operational Supervisor Observers rated controller performance on an 8-point scale (see Appendix D) where higher scores denoted better performance. We compared observer ratings obtained in the enhanced condition to the ratings obtained in the control condition on an item-by-item basis for each enhancement condition. Though the mean ratings were often in the expected direction, with higher ratings for the enhanced conditions than the control, the differences were not statistically significant for the En Route, Arrival, and All Enhancements scenarios.

We found several rating differences to be statistically significant for the SUA scenarios. Ratings of overall safe and efficient traffic flow were significantly higher when the SUA enhancement was used ($M = 7.4, SD = 0.5$) than in the control condition ($M = 5.9, SD = 1.4$), $F(1, 6) = 7.71$, $p < .05$. The ratings for using control instructions effectively/efficiently were also higher for the enhanced ($M = 7.5, SD = 0.5$) than the control condition ($M = 5.9, SD = 1.8$), $F(1, 6) = 7.57$, $p < .05$.

For three of the SUA items, the differences approached significance. The ratings for overall attention and situation awareness were marginally higher for the enhanced condition ($M = 7.5$, $SD = 0.5$) than the control ($M = 6.5, SD = 1.1$), $F(1, 6) = 4.80, p = .07$. Similarly, ratings for ensuring positive control (i.e., tailoring control actions to the situation and using effective procedures for handling heavy or unusual traffic situations) were marginally higher for the enhanced condition ($M = 7.5$, $SD = 0.8$) than the control ($M = 5.6$, $SD = 1.9$), $F(1, 6) = 5.00$, $p = .07$. Finally, ratings for overall prioritizing were marginally higher for the enhanced condition ($M = 7.6$, $SD = 0.5$) than the control ($M = 6.3$, $SD = 1.4$), $F(1, 6) = 5.11$, $p = .06$.

3.10 Observer Post-Scenario Questionnaire

For the SUA scenarios, the Operational Supervisor Observers rated controllers as more effective in complying with SUA restrictions when the SUA enhancement was used ($M = 7.5$, $SD = 0.9$) than in the control condition ($M = 5.0$, $SD = 2.0$), $F(1, 6) = 9.38$, $p < .05$.

For the Arrival scenarios, observers rated controller workload lower in the Arrival 1 scenario ($M = 6.3$, $SD = 0.5$) than Arrival 2 ($M = 7.0$, $SD = 0.5$), $F(1, 6) = 9.00$, $p < .05$. They also rated the traffic complexity of Arrival 1 ($M = 6.5$, $SD = 0.5$) as lower than that of Arrival 2 ($M = 7.0$, $SD = 0.5$), $F(1, 6) = 8.00$, $p < .05$.

3.11 Participant Post-Scenario Questionnaire

The Participant Post-Scenario Questionnaire (see Appendix F) contained two parts. The first nine questions asked controllers to rate the workload and complexity of the scenario. The controllers were to answer only the remaining questions if the scenario used enhancements and asked how the enhancement(s) affected various aspects of their performance.

For the first nine items, we were able to compare ratings for scenarios in the experimental conditions with those in the control conditions. We calculated mean ratings on an item-by-item basis and analyzed the differences between the enhanced and control conditions. We present the mean ratings for mental workload in Table 9. Ratings were provided on an 8-point scale (1 = low and 8 = high). There were no significant differences between ratings for the enhanced and control conditions for any of the enhancement conditions. For the SUA scenarios, ratings of physical workload were lower for the SUA 1 scenario ($M = 3.3$, $SD = 1.9$) than SUA 2 ($M = 4.9$, $SD = 1.9$), $F(1, 6) = 26.68$, $p < .01$. Ratings of scenario difficulty were also lower for SUA 1 ($M = 4.3$, $SD = 1.9$) than SUA 2 ($M = 5.3$, $SD = 1.6$), $F(1, 6) = 6.40$, $p < .05$.

Table 9. Mean Ratings (and Standard Deviations) of Overall Mental Workload

Enhancement Condition	Enhanced	Control
En Route	4.4 (0.7)	4.5 (2.0)
Arrival	4.4 (2.1)	4.9 (1.4)
SUA	5.4 (1.6)	5.5 (2.0)
All Enhancements	6.1 (1.5)	6.4 (1.1)

Many of the questionnaire items showed patterns of ratings in the expected direction. Examples include lower workload and lower complexity ratings for scenarios where enhancements were used than the control scenarios, but these differences were not statistically significant. One item in particular showed a consistent pattern for all enhancement conditions. Ratings of mental workload were always lower for the enhanced conditions than the control. This pattern approached significance ($p = .06$).

Controllers completed the remaining questionnaire items only for those scenarios that used enhancements. Controllers rated how the display enhancements affected their ability to accomplish the specified task on an 8-point scale (1 = interfered and 8 = helped). For those questions, we calculated mean ratings for each enhancement condition. Table 10 lists the mean ratings for each item. Ratings of 4.5 or above indicate that the enhancements helped the controllers accomplish ATC tasks.

Table 10. Mean Ratings (and Standard Deviations) for Each Item by Enhancement Condition

Task	En Route	Arrival	SUA	All
Plan ahead	5.8 (1.1)	7.1 (1.8)	7.1 (1.9)	6.5 (1.0)
Maintain Attention	5.4 (1.4)	6.9 (1.2)	6.9 (1.0)	6.1 (1.3)
Maintain situational awareness	5.8 (1.8)	7.0 (1.2)	7.0 (1.1)	6.0 (1.1)
Maintain safe traffic flow	5.6 (2.0)	6.5 (1.2)	6.5 (1.0)	6.0 (1.2)
Maintain efficient traffic flow	5.8 (1.9)	5.6 (1.4)	5.6 (2.0)	6.4 (1.4)
Prioritize control actions	5.3 (1.5)	7.1 (1.2)	7.1 (2.0)	6.4 (1.2)
Detect aircraft heading to different destinations	5.4 (1.7)	5.6 (0.8)	5.6 (1.0)	7.5 (1.4)
Meet restrictions in a timely manner	4.4 (1.7)	5.3 (1.1)	5.3 (1.7)	6.4 (0.8)

3.12 Participant Exit Questionnaire

The Exit Questionnaire asked controllers to rate their overall experience with the enhancements during the study. On an 8-point scale (1 = interfered, 8 = helped), controller ratings indicated that the enhancements helped somewhat in maintaining safe traffic flow ($M = 6.9$, $SD = 1.3$), efficient traffic flow ($M = 6.6$, $SD = 1.2$), attention ($M = 6.9$, $SD = 1.1$), and situation awareness ($M = 6.8$, $SD = 1.2$). Controllers also reported that the enhancements helped somewhat in prioritizing control actions ($M = 6.6$, $SD = 0.9$) and planning ahead ($M = 6.9$, $SD = 0.8$).

When asked to rate how each enhancement affected display complexity, traffic complexity, and cognitive complexity, controllers reported that each of the enhancements taken individually reduced complexity, with the overflight enhancement having the smallest effect. For the All Enhancements scenarios, where all of the enhancements were used at the same time, the ratings indicated a slight increase in display complexity and no effect on either traffic or cognitive complexity. Table 11 lists the mean ratings for each enhancement (1 = decreased, 8 = increased).

Table 11. Mean Ratings of the Enhancements Effect on Display, Traffic, and Cognitive Complexity

Enhancement	Display Complexity M (SD)	Traffic Complexity M (SD)	Cognitive Complexity M (SD)
Destination Airport	3.5 (1.4)	3.3 (1.7)	3.0 (2.1)
Overflight	4.9 (1.6)	4.2 (0.8)	4.0 (1.3)
SUA	3.4 (1.4)	3.4 (1.7)	3.0 (2.1)
All Enhancements	5.3 (2.0)	4.6 (2.1)	4.4 (2.7)

4. Discussion

With each enhancement tested, we found some significant effects on controller performance. When we added the overflight enhancement to the En Route scenarios, controllers issued fewer altitude clearances overall, suggesting more efficient traffic flow. With the destination airport enhancement, we found that controllers issued fewer altitude clearances for the arrival aircraft. Though the SUA enhancement did not affect any of the objective measures we collected, our Operational Supervisor Observers perceived that the controllers were more effective at complying with the SUA restrictions and were better able to handle heavy or unusual traffic with the SUA enhancement. Overall, these data suggest that enhancing the existing displays by selectively highlighting relevant information may improve efficiency and safety of air traffic operations.

Several of the measures we collected reflected efficiency. Air traffic measures such as the number of clearances issued to aircraft are one objective indicator of controller efficiency. Reductions in the numbers of altitude or heading changes can be indicative of more efficient operations. The number of operational errors is often used as a measure of air traffic safety. In this study, the controllers made very few operational errors, making the measure insensitive. Remarks made by Operational Supervisor Observers about controller performance and situational awareness provided some indications that safety was positively affected by the enhancements.

We obtained these results when we tested each of the enhancements separately. In an applied setting, however, controllers may want to use several enhancements at the same time. We designed the All Enhancements condition to test what happens to controller performance when all of the enhancements are present on the display at once. One undesirable effect may have been clutter on the display and increased display complexity. Controller ratings in the Exit Questionnaire indicated a slight increase in display complexity, but we did not observe any decrements in any of our other measures for the All Enhancements condition. However, we did not find the beneficial effects that we observed when we tested the enhancements individually. Cardosi and Hannon (1999) stressed the importance of testing the application of color coding with the specific tasks and in the environment that it is designed to support.

We designed the enhancements to mitigate complexity factors in ATC (Ahlstrom, Rubinstein et al., 2001). It was difficult to assess whether the enhancements were effective in reducing complexity because definitions of complexity vary and we do not have any good measures of overall complexity. There are several metrics for assessing air traffic complexity, such as the Dynamic Density measure (Laudeman, Shelden, Branstrom, & Brasil, 1998). Unfortunately, these metrics are still being developed and validated. The participants' ratings of how the enhancements affected complexity suggest that the enhancements were somewhat effective.

Some of the complexity factors identified by Mogford et al. (1995) were due to the presence of altitude and airspace restrictions. The analysis of how well the controllers complied with the various restrictions in this study did not result in the expected findings. One of the anticipated benefits of the enhancements was better compliance with restrictions. However, we failed to find any differences in that factor between the enhanced and control conditions. Further review of the data revealed that the controllers were actually very effective in complying with the restrictions at all times, creating a range restriction in the data. Controllers regularly deal with such restrictions in the field, where non-compliance has repercussions. Routing an aircraft through active SUA, for example, is considered a deviation in the field and is treated very seriously by the controllers and their supervisors. Even with the added complexity of various patterns of SUA activation, our participants were very good at keeping aircraft out of the restricted areas. Similarly, they were effective in meeting altitude and MIT restrictions.

We created two similar scenarios for each enhancement condition to allow participants to experience both the experimental conditions, enhanced and control, while avoiding learning effects. Even though we developed these scenarios to be similar, we found significant differences between scenarios for some of our measures. The differences we observed may be due to the inherent characteristics of the scenarios themselves or due to the controllers' manipulation of the traffic. Because of the dynamic nature of ATC, the same controller may work with the same traffic sample and end up with different outcomes. However, if the differences are due to the characteristics of the scenarios themselves, the factor of scenario may interact with the experimental condition. It is possible that a characteristic present in only one of the two scenarios made the enhancement more or less useful. We adopted the Latin Square design to mitigate these effects, but because this is not a completely crossed design, we did not analyze the data for any such interactions (Myers & Well, 1991).

4.1 Display Enhancements Decision Task

The Display Enhancements Decision Task results revealed several interesting findings. As expected, the participants were significantly faster in responding to the airport question when we used the Destination Airport enhancement. Interestingly, their response times were also faster when we enhanced the incorrect data block. It seems that the enhancement facilitated the processing of the airport identifier in both cases.

Given these findings, we expected to observe a similar pattern of results for the question that asked which aircraft was at a particular altitude. For the altitude question however, there were no differences in response times between the three conditions. We did not observe an advantage in selecting a data block that listed a specified altitude when the altitude was colored. There are several plausible explanations for the lack of an effect.

It may be that the destination airport enhancement provided information that is more useful by using the color coding redundantly. There were two possible airport identifiers: one was magenta, the other, cyan. The overflight enhancement used color to highlight an area in the data block, but, in this task, it did not convey any additional information. The color was irrelevant to the task of answering the question. It only served to focus attention on a field in the data block. The advantages observed with the destination airport enhancement may be a result of the participants using the information conveyed by the color coding to process and discriminate the information more quickly.

Another possible explanation of the disparate findings is that the color we selected (green) was not as effective at drawing the controllers' attention as the colors used for the airport identifiers (magenta and cyan). However, if the participants were using the strategy we described previously, any color that was perceptually distinguishable from the data block color should have produced the same effect.

4.2 Map Test

We designed GEN for this study based on the geographical layout of the United States. The average score on the Map Test was above 75%, indicating that even after 1 day of training, most controllers were familiar with the Genera Low sector, its SUA, airports, and fixes. Providing simulation participants with airspace that is easily learned is a great advantage that reduces training time. Using generic airspace provides the additional advantage of being able to draw on controllers from facilities around the country (Guttman & Stein, 1997; Guttman et al., 1995).

5. Conclusions

The use of color radar displays at ATC facilities makes the implementation and use of color enhancements possible. The application of color to a display can have both positive and detrimental effects, depending on how the color is used and on the task to be performed. The present study examined the application of color display enhancements to specific air traffic situations. Ahlstrom, Rubinstein et al. (2001) designed the enhancements to address areas that contribute to ATC complexity. We hypothesized that by making useful information more readily available to the controller, we could reduce the effects of these complexity factors and observe improvements in controller performance. We tested this hypothesis in a high fidelity, human-in-the-loop simulation. Overall, the results suggest that the enhancements improved efficiency and safety of air traffic operations.

Our finding that beneficial effects of the enhancements are lost when they are presented simultaneously provides an important caution. There are many efforts underway to develop tools for ATC. Most tools are designed and evaluated independently. Assuming that several tools will be selected for deployment to the field, the critical test for each tool will be to evaluate its effectiveness in an integrated environment.

We were cautious in selecting the colors for the enhancements and in the application of the colors to the display. We wanted to reduce the potential for introducing disruptive effects due to the use of color. For example, people have more difficulty integrating information from display elements that are of different colors (Wickens & Andre, 1990). Controllers integrate information from aircraft data blocks to maintain situational awareness and detect potential conflicts. We would not want the enhancements to affect their ability to perform these critical tasks. On the other hand, we wanted the application of color to highlight information on the radar display. To accomplish this, the color must be discriminable from other elements on the display. For this reason, we based our selection of colors on existing guidelines (e.g., Cardosi & Hannon, 1999).

One of the enhancements, the destination airport enhancement, used color as a redundant cue. That is to say that the aircraft data blocks were already coded for destination airport with the airport identifier. The application of the enhancement provided an additional coding by color. The other enhancements did not use color as a redundant cue. The results of the Display Enhancements Decision Task suggest that there may be important differences in how redundantly coded enhancements affect information processing as compared to non-redundant enhancements. The redundantly coded destination airport enhancement produced faster response times; however, the non-redundant overflight enhancement had no effect on controller performance.

This study used a Latin Square design for counterbalancing and experimental control. The design does not provide for the analysis of possible interactions between factors. Though we tried to make the paired scenarios similar for each enhancement condition, the data suggest that there may have been important differences between the scenarios, particularly in the Arrival condition. This should be an important consideration in future simulations. One approach is to develop paired traffic samples but include a process to determine how similar they are. This may be accomplished by applying a metric that evaluates the complexity of the airspace such as a dynamic density measure (Laudeman et al., 1998). Another approach is to manipulate the factor by developing traffic samples of varying traffic complexity and analyzing the effects of this factor and its interaction with the factor of interest.

One measure that we did not collect in this study is visual scanning. This measure may be more sensitive to some of the effects of the enhancements than the measures we collected. If an enhancement was distracting and continually disrupted the controllers' scan of the radar display, the visual scanning data would provide direct evidence of such an effect. The measures we collected, however, would only show indirect, reduced effects, such as reduced ratings of controller situational awareness or increased ratings of cognitive workload.

This was an exploratory study with a small number of participants. However, the study provided an initial glimpse into the possible benefits of using color on ATC displays. There are probably other enhancements and alternative information coding techniques beyond what we explored (e.g., using other colors or using color as a redundant cue). Further research is needed to address the questions of which enhancements are most beneficial and what is the most effective implementation. Until there is clearer guidance on these complex issues, caution should be exercised in developing future enhancements or air traffic tools that add color to the radar display.

References

Ahlstrom, V., & Longo, K. (2001). *Human factors design guide update (Report number DOT/FAA/CT-96/01): A revision to Chapter 8 – Computer Human Interface Guidelines* (DOT/FAA/CT-01/08). Atlantic City International Airport, NJ: FAA Technical Center.

Ahlstrom, U., Rubinstein, J., Siegel, S., Mogford, R., & Manning, C. (2001). *Display concepts for en route air traffic control* (DOT/FAA/CT-TN01/06). Atlantic City International Airport, NJ: FAA William J. Hughes Technical Center.

Buckley, E. P., DeBaryshe, B. D., Hitchner, N., & Kohn, P. (1983). *Methods and measurements in real-time air traffic control system simulation* (DOT/FAA/CT83/26). Atlantic City International Airport, NJ: FAA William J. Hughes Technical Center.

Cardosi, K., & Hannon, D. (1999). *Guidelines for the use of color in ATC displays* (DOT/FAA/AR-99/52). Washington, DC: Office of Aviation Research.

Christ, R. E. (1975). Review and analysis of color-coding research for visual displays. *Human Factors, 17*, 542-570.

Cook, T. C. (1974). *Color coding – A review of the literature.* Aberdeen Proving Ground, MD: U.S. Army Human Engineering Laboratory.

D'Arcy, J., & Della Rocco, P. S. (2001). *Air Traffic Control Specialist decision making and strategic planning – A field survey* (DOT/FAA/CT-TN01/05). Atlantic City International Airport, NJ: FAA William J. Hughes Technical Center.

Graham, R. V., Young, D., Pichancourt, I., Marsden, A., & Irkitz, A. (1994). *ODID IV report* (Report Number 269/94). Eurocontrol Experimental Centre.

Guttman, J., & Stein, E. S. (1997). *En route generic airspace evaluation* (DOT/FAA/CT-TN97/7). Atlantic City International Airport, NJ: FAA William J. Hughes Technical Center.

Guttman, J., Stein, E. S., & Gromelski, S. (1995). *The influence of generic airspace on Air Traffic Controller performance* (DOT/FAA/CT-TN95/38). Atlantic City International Airport, NJ: FAA Technical Center.

Ishihara, S. (1997). *Ishihara's tests for colour-deficiency.* Tokyo: Kanehara & Co., Ltd.

Krois, P., & Marsden, A. (1997). *FAA ODID IV: En route baseline comparison simulation final report* (Crown Document Number C012-001-008). Washington, DC: Crown Communications.

Laudeman, I. V., Shelden, S. G., Branstrom, R., & Brasil, C. L. (1998). *Dynamic density: An air traffic management metric* (NASA-TM-1998-112226). Ames Research Center.

Mayhew, D. J. (1992). *Principles and guidelines in software user interface design.* New Jersey: Prentice-Hall.

Mogford, R. H., Guttman, J. A., Morrow, S. L., & Kopardekar, P. (1995). *The complexity construct in air traffic control: A review and synthesis of the literature* (DOT/FAA/CT-TN95/22). Atlantic City International Airport, NJ: FAA Technical Center.

Mogford, R. H., Murphy, E. D., Roske-Hofstrand, R. J., Yastrop, G., & Guttman, J. A. (1994). *Research techniques for documenting cognitive processes in air traffic control: Sector complexity and decision making* (DOT/FAA/CT-TN94/3). Atlantic City International Airport, NJ: FAA Technical Center.

Myers, J. L., & Well, A. D. (1991). *Research design and statistical analysis.* New York: Harper Collins.

Remington, R. W., Johnston, J. C., & Ruthruff, E. (2000). Visual search in complex displays: Factors affecting conflict detection by Air Traffic Controllers. *Human Factors, 42*(3), 349-366.

Reynolds, L. (1994). Colour for air traffic control displays. *Displays, 15*(4), 215-225.

Skiles, T., Graham, R., Marsden, A., & Krois, P. (1997). En route ODID-PVD baseline comparisons. *Journal of Air Traffic Control, 39*(1), 38-41.

Sollenberger, R. L., Stein, E. S., & Gromelski, S. (1996). *The development and evaluation of a behaviorally based rating form for the assessment of Air Traffic Controller performance* (DOT/FAA/CT-TN96/16). Atlantic City International Airport, NJ: FAA William J. Hughes Technical Center.

Stein, E. S. (1985). *Air Traffic Controller workload: An examination of workload probe* (DOT/FAA/CT-TN84/24). Atlantic City International Airport, NJ. Federal Aviation Administration Technical Center.

Stein, E. S. (1991). Evaluating Air Traffic Controller workload using real time person in the loop simulation. *Journal of Air Traffic Control, 33*(4), 55-58.

Stein, E. S. (1992). *Air traffic control visual scanning* (DOT/FAA/CT-TN92/16). Atlantic City International Airport, NJ: FAA Technical Center.

Triesman, A. (1986). Properties, parts, and objects. In K. R. Boff, L. Kaufman, & J. P. Thomas (Eds.), *Handbook of perception and human performance.* New York: Wiley.

Triesman, A., & Gelade, G. (1980). A feature integration theory of attention. *Cognitive Psychology, 12*, 97-136.

Vardaman, J. J., & Stein, E. S. (1998). *The development and evaluation of a behaviorally based rating form for the assessment of en route Air Traffic Controller performance* (DOT/FAA/CT-TN98/5). Atlantic City International Airport, NJ: FAA William J. Hughes Technical Center.

Wickens, C. D., & Andre, A. D. (1990). Proximity compatibility and information display: Effects of color, space, and objectness on information integration. *Human Factors, 32*(1), 61-77.

Wickens, C. D., & Hollands, J. G. (2000). *Engineering psychology and human performance* (3rd ed.). Upper Saddle River, NJ: Prentice Hall.

Wickens, C. D., Mavor, A. S., & McGee, J. P. (Eds.). (1997). *Flight to the future, human factors in air traffic control.* Washington, DC: National Academy Press.

Wickens, C. D., Mavor, A. S., Parasuraman, R., & McGee, J. P. (Eds.). (1998). *The future of air traffic control, human operators and automation.* Washington, DC: National Academy Press.

Acronyms

ANOVA	Analyses of Variance
ARTCC	Air Route Traffic Control Center
ATC	Air Traffic Control
ATCS	Air Traffic Control Specialist
ATWIT	Air Traffic Workload Input Technique
CAMI	Civil Aerospace Medical Institute
CPC	Certified Professional Controller
CRD	Computer Readout Device
DC	Display Controls
DESIREE	Distributed Environment for Simulation, Rapid Engineering, and Experimentation
DSR	Display System Replacement
FAA	Federal Aviation Administration
MIT	Miles-in-Trail
NAS	National Airspace System
ODID	Operational Display and Input Development
RDHFL	Research Development and Human Factors Laboratory
RT	Response Time
STARS	Standard Terminal Automation Replacement System
SUA	Special Use Airspace
TGF	Target Generation Facility
WJHTC	William J. Hughes Technical Center

Appendix A
Informed Consent Form

Display Enhancements Project

I, _____, give my informed consent to participate in the study entitled "Display Enhancements for En Route Air Traffic Control.

Nature and Purpose

I have been recruited to volunteer as a participant in the project named above. The purpose of the study is to investigate how enhancements to the radar display can be used to reduce complexity for air traffic controllers. The research team will use the data gathered from this simulation to provide input on the viability of developing and implementing enhancements to the presentation of data which will work to decrease air traffic airspace complexity.

Experimental Procedures

Participants will control simulated air traffic in eight different scenarios under two different experimental conditions. One condition (four scenarios) will use display enhancements, the other (four scenarios) will not. An automated data collection system will record important simulation events and produce a set of system effectiveness measures. In addition, ATCS observers (SATCSs) will make over-the-shoulder observations to evaluate the controller's effectiveness with and without the display enhancements. After each scenario, controllers will complete questionnaires to evaluate the benefits of display enhancements. The simulation will be audio-video recorded for the purposes of post experiment content analysis of controller communications.

Discomforts and Risks

I understand that I will not be exposed to any foreseeable risks or intrusive measurement techniques.

Benefits

I understand that the only direct benefit to me is that I will have the opportunity to provide valuable feedback and insight on the feasibility of using display enhancements to reduce ATC complexity.

Participant's Responsibilities

I am aware that to participate in this study that I am required to have 1) normal color vision, 2) 20/30 normal or corrected-to-normal vision, and 3) not to be on any medical waiver. During the experiment, it will be my responsibility to control the simulated air traffic as if I was controlling traffic at my home facility. I will answer any questions asked during the experiment to the best of my abilities.

Participant's Assurances

I understand that my participation in this study is strictly **voluntary**. I am free to withdraw at any time without penalty or consequences to my job or my employment. I understand that my data are strictly **confidential**. I may request that my data not be used. No individual names or identities will be recorded or released in any reports. Dr. Tanya Yuditsky has adequately answered any questions I have about this study, my participation, and the procedures involved. I understand that Dr. Yuditsky will be available to answer any questions concerning procedures throughout this study. I understand that if new findings develop during the course of this research that may relate to my decision to continue to participation, I will be informed.

I have not given up any of my legal rights or released any individual or institution from liability for negligence.

I also understand that the researcher of this study may terminate my participation if she feels this to be in my best interest. If I have questions about this study or need to report any adverse effects from the research procedures, I will contact Dr. Tanya Yuditsky, Project Coordinator, FAA William J. Hughes Technical Center, at (609) 485-5375.

I have read this consent document. I understand its contents, and I freely consent to participate in this study under the conditions described. I have received a copy of this consent form.

Research Participant: _____   Date: _____

Investigator: _____   Date: _____

Witness: _____   Date: _____

Appendix B
Controller Background Questionnaire

Display Enhancements
Background Information Form

This questionnaire is designed to obtain information about your background as an Air Traffic Control Specialist. The information will be used to describe the participants in this study as a group. Your identity will remain anonymous.

Controller or Observer (*circle one*)   Participant Code _____

Male or Female (*circle one*)

Age Range: (*check one*)

__18-30   __31-35   __36-40   __41-45   __46-50   __51-55

1. What is your total experience as an Air Traffic Control Specialist (include both FAA and military experience)?

    Years:_____ Months:_____

2. How long have you actively controlled traffic for the FAA?

    Years:_____ Months:_____

3. How long have you been a Certified Professional Controller (CPC)?

    Years:_____ Months:_____

4. How long have you actively controlled traffic in the en route environment?

    Years:_____ Months:_____

5. How long have you been using DSR?

    Years:_____ Months:_____

6. Please describe the type of traffic you work in your area of specialization by assigning a percentage to the following:

    _____ transitional traffic to a major airport

    _____ high altitude en route (flight level 240 and above)

    _____ low altitude en route (flight level 230 and below)

7. Does your area of specialization contain special use or restricted airspace?

    __ YES   __ NO

    IF YES, HOW OFTEN DOES IT BECOME ACTIVE? (E.G., DAILY) _____

Appendix C

Procedures for Measuring the CIE Chromaticity Coordinates of the Enhancement Colors

We used the fast scanning, Photo Research PR-650 spectroradiometric telecolorimeter to measure the CIE and luminance values of the colors used for the enhancements. To obtain accurate luminance/radiance or color measurements, the measuring area of the lens should cover approximately half to three quarters of the area of interest in the target. Because our targets were fairly small lines, we created color solids that were approximately half-inch squares for the measurement process and used a SL-1X Supplementary Close-up lens with a "black spot" size of 0.052 inches (1.38mm). We first adjusted the focus of the colorimeter by focusing the vertical centerline of the aperture on a white piece of paper. The PR-650 was secured in place with a tripod. Looking through the viewing eyepiece, the PR-650 was aligned and focused on the target to be measured.

Measures taken were of four colors: red, cyan, magenta, and green. The measurements were repeated in each of the four quadrants of the DSR screen: upper left, upper right, lower left and lower right. The output included the x,y coordinates (1931 CIE Chromatic Diagram), the u' and v' measures (1976 CIE Chromatic Diagram) and the candelas per meter squared (luminance).

Over-The-Shoulder Observer Questionnaire

Subject Matter Expert Observer Rating Form

Observer Code _____   Date _____

Controller _____   Scenario _____

INSTRUCTIONS

This form is designed to be used by supervisory Air Traffic Control Specialists to evaluate the effectiveness of controllers working in simulation environments. SATCSs will observe and rate the performance of controllers in several different performance dimensions using the scale below as a general purpose guide. Use the entire scale range as much as possible. You will see a wide range of controller performance. Take extensive notes on what you see. Do not depend on your memory. Write down your observations. Space is provided after each scale for comments. You may make preliminary ratings during the course of the scenario. However, wait until the scenario is finished before making your final ratings and remain flexible until the end when you have had an opportunity to see all the available behavior. At all times please focus on what you actually see and hear. This includes what the controller does and what you might reasonably infer from the actions of the pilots. Try to avoid inferring what you think may be happening. If you do not observe relevant behavior or the results of that behavior, then you may leave a specific rating blank. Also, please write down any comments that may help improve this evaluation form. Do not write your name on the form itself. Your identity will remain anonymous, as your data will be identified by an observer code known only to yourself and the researchers conducting this study. The observations you make do not need to be restricted to the performance areas covered in this form and may include other areas that you think are important.

ASSUMPTIONS

ATC is a complex activity that contains both observable and unobservable behavior. There are so many complex behaviors involved that no observational rating form can cover everything. A sample of the behaviors is the best that can be achieved, and a good form focuses on those behaviors that controllers themselves have identified as the most relevant in terms of their overall performance. Most controller performance is at or above the minimum standards regarding safety and efficiency. The goal of the rating system is to differentiate performance above this minimum. The lowest rating should be assigned for meeting minimum standards and also for anything below the minimum since this should be a rare event. It is important for the observer/rater to feel comfortable using the entire scale and to understand that all ratings should be based on behavior that is actually observed.

Rating Scale Descriptors

Remove this Page and keep it available while doing ratings

SCALE	QUALITY	SUPPLEMENTARY
1	**Least Effective**	Unconfident, Indecisive, Inefficient, Disorganized, Behind the power curve, Rough, Leaves some tasks incomplete, Makes mistakes
2	**Poor**	May issue conflicting instructions, Doesn't plan completely
3	**Fair**	Distracted between tasks
4	**Low Satisfactory**	Postpones routine actions
5	**High Satisfactory**	Knows the job fairly well
6	**Good**	Works steadily, Solves most problems
7	**Very Good**	Knows the job thoroughly, Plans well
8	**Most Effective**	Confident, Decisive, Efficient, Organized, Ahead of the power curve, Smooth, Completes all necessary tasks, Makes no mistakes

I - MAINTAINING SAFE AND EFFICIENT TRAFFIC FLOW

1. Maintaining Separation and Resolving Potential Conflicts............ **1 2 3 4 5 6 7 8**
   - using control instructions that maintain appropriate aircraft and airspace separation
   - detecting and resolving impending conflicts early
   - recognizing the need for speed restrictions and wake turbulence separation
   Comments:

2. Sequencing Aircraft Efficiently.. **1 2 3 4 5 6 7 8**
   - using efficient and orderly spacing techniques for arrival, departure, and en route aircraft
   - maintaining safe arrival and departure intervals that minimize delays
   Comments:

3. Using Control Instructions Effectively/Efficiently.......................... **1 2 3 4 5 6 7 8**
   - providing accurate navigational assistance to pilots
   - issuing economical clearances that result in need for few additional instructions to handle aircraft completely
   - ensuring clearances use minimum necessary flight path changes
   Comments:

4. Overall Safe and Efficient Traffic Flow Scale Rating.................... **1 2 3 4 5 6 7 8**
   Comments:

II - MAINTAINING ATTENTION AND SITUATION AWARENESS

5. Maintaining Awareness of Aircraft Positions **1 2 3 4 5 6 7 8**
   - avoiding fixation on one area of the radar scope when other areas need attention
   - using scanning patterns that monitor all aircraft on the radar scope

   Comments:

6. Ensuring Positive Control... **1 2 3 4 5 6 7 8**
   - tailoring control actions to situation
   - using effective procedures for handling heavy, emergency, and unusual traffic situations

   Comments:

7. Detecting Pilot Deviations from Control Instructions.................... **1 2 3 4 5 6 7 8**
   - ensuring that pilots follow assigned clearances correctly
   - correcting pilot deviations in a timely manner

   Comments:

8. Correcting Own Errors in a Timely Manner **1 2 3 4 5 6 7 8**
   - acting quickly to correct errors
   - changing an issued clearance when necessary to expedite traffic flow

   Comments:

9. Overall Attention and Situation Awareness Scale Rating.............. **1 2 3 4 5 6 7 8**
   Comments:

III – PRIORITIZING

10. Taking Actions in an Appropriate Order of Importance **1 2 3 4 5 6 7 8**
    - resolving situations that need immediate attention before
      handling low priority tasks
    - issuing control instructions in a prioritized, structured, and
      timely manner
    Comments:

11. Preplanning Control Actions **1 2 3 4 5 6 7 8**
    - scanning adjacent sectors to plan for future and conflicting
      traffic
    - studying pending flight strips in bay
    Comments:

12. Handling Control Tasks for Several Aircraft **1 2 3 4 5 6 7 8**
    - shifting control tasks between several aircraft when necessary
    - communicating in timely fashion while sharing time with
      other actions
    Comments:

13. Marking Flight Strips while Performing Other Tasks.................... **1 2 3 4 5 6 7 8**
    - marking flight strips accurately while talking or performing
      other tasks
    - keeping flight strips current
    Comments:

14. Overall Prioritizing Scale Rating.. **1 2 3 4 5 6 7 8**
    Comments:

IV – PROVIDING CONTROL INFORMATION

15. Providing Essential Air Traffic Control Information **1 2 3 4 5 6 7 8**
    - providing mandatory services and advisories to pilots in a timely manner
    - exchanging essential information
    Comments:

16. Providing Additional Air Traffic Control Information................... **1 2 3 4 5 6 7 8**
    - providing additional services when workload is not a factor
    - exchanging additional information
    Comments:

17. Providing Coordination **1 2 3 4 5 6 7 8**
    - providing effective and timely coordination
    - using proper point-out procedures
    Comments:

18. Overall Providing Control Information Scale Rating.....................**1 2 3 4 5 6 7 8**
    Comments:

V – TECHNICAL KNOWLEDGE

19. Showing Knowledge of LOAs and SOPs.......................................1 2 3 4 5 6 7 8
    - controlling traffic as depicted in current LOAs and SOPs
    - performing handoff procedures correctly
    Comments:

20a. Showing Knowledge of Aircraft Capabilities and Limitations 1 2 3 4 5 6 7 8
    - using appropriate speed, vectoring, and/or altitude
        assignments to separate aircraft with varied flight capabilities
    - issuing clearances that are within aircraft performance
        parameters
    Comments:

20b. Showing Effective Use of Equipment 1 2 3 4 5 6 7 8
    - updating data blocks
    - using equipment capabilities
    Comments:

21. Overall Technical Knowledge Scale Rating................................... 1 2 3 4 5 6 7 8
    Comments:

VI – COMMUNICATING

22. Using Proper Phraseology **1 2 3 4 5 6 7 8**
    • using words and phrases specified in the 7110.65
    • using phraseology that is appropriate for the situation
    • using minimum necessary verbiage
    Comments:

23. Communicating Clearly and Efficiently **1 2 3 4 5 6 7 8**
    • speaking at the proper volume and rate for pilots to understand
    • speaking fluently while scanning or performing other tasks
    • ensuring clearance delivery is complete, correct and timely
    • speaking with confident, authoritative tone of voice
    Comments:

24. Listening to Pilot Readbacks and Requests **1 2 3 4 5 6 7 8**
    • correcting pilot readback errors
    • acknowledging pilot or other controller requests promptly
    • processing requests correctly in a timely manner
    Comments:

25. Overall Communicating Scale Rating **1 2 3 4 5 6 7 8**
    Comments:

Appendix E

Observer Post-Scenario Questionnaire

Participant Code _____   Scenario _____

For the questions below, please circle the number that best describes your experience in this scenario. Please also provide comments to elaborate your responses whenever possible.

1. How did the Display Enhancements affect the controller's ability to maintain safe traffic flow?

1 ------ 2 ------ 3 ------ 4 ------ 5 ------ 6 ------ 7
interfered   no effect   helped

Comments:

2. How did the Display Enhancements affect the controller's ability to maintain efficient traffic flow?

1 ------ 2 ------ 3 ------ 4 ------ 5 ------ 6 ------ 7
interfered   no effect   helped

Comments:

3. How did the Display Enhancements affect the controller's ability to maintain attention?

1 ------ 2 ------ 3 ------ 4 ------ 5 ------ 6 ------ 7
interfered   no effect   helped

Comments:

4. How did the Display Enhancements affect the controller's ability to maintain situation awareness?

1 ------ 2 ------ 3 ------ 4 ------ 5 ------ 6 ------ 7
interfered   no effect   helped

Comments:

5. How did the Display Enhancements affect the controller's ability to prioritize control actions?

1 ------ 2 ------ 3 ------ 4 ------ 5 ------ 6 ------ 7
interfered   no effect   helped

Comments:

6. How did the Display Enhancements affect the controller's ability to plan ahead?

1 ------ 2 ------ 3 ------ 4 ------ 5 ------ 6 ------ 7
interfered   no effect   helped

Comments:

Participant Post-Scenario Questionnaire

Participant Code _____   Scenario _____

For the questions below, please circle the number that best describes your experience **in this scenario**.

1. How realistic was the simulation?

   1 ----- 2 ----- 3 ----- 4 ----- 5 ----- 6 ----- 7 ----- 8

   unrealistic   average   realistic

2. How hard were you working during this scenario?

   1 ----- 2 ----- 3 ----- 4 ----- 5 ----- 6 ----- 7 ----- 8

   not hard   average   very hard

3. How would you rate your mental workload in this scenario?

   1 ----- 2 ----- 3 ----- 4 ----- 5 ----- 6 ----- 7 ----- 8

   low   moderate   high

4. How would you rate your physical workload in this scenario?

   1 ----- 2 ----- 3 ----- 4 ----- 5 ----- 6 ----- 7 ----- 8

   low   moderate   high

5. How would you rate your overall (mental and physical) workload in this scenario?

   1 ----- 2 ----- 3 ----- 4 ----- 5 ----- 6 ----- 7 ----- 8

   low   moderate   high

6. How difficult was this scenario?

   1 ----- 2 ----- 3 ----- 4 ----- 5 ----- 6 ----- 7 ----- 8

   not difficult   average   very difficult

7. How well did you manage traffic during this scenario?

   1 ----- 2 ----- 3 ----- 4 ----- 5 ----- 6 ----- 7 ----- 8

   not well   borderline   very well

8. How would you rate the traffic complexity of this problem?

   1 ----- 2 ----- 3 ----- 4 ----- 5 ----- 6 ----- 7 ----- 8

   not complex   average   very complex

9. How would you rate the display complexity of the problem?

   1 ----- 2 ----- 3 ----- 4 ----- 5 ----- 6 ----- 7 ----- 8

   not complex   average   very complex

For scenarios that used Display Enhancements, please answer questions 10 – 19 below. For scenarios that did not use Display Enhancements, proceed to question 20.

10. How did the Display Enhancements affect your ability to plan ahead in this scenario?

1 ----- 2 ----- 3 ----- 4 ----- 5 ----- 6 ----- 7 ----- 8

interfered   no effect   helped

11. How did the Display Enhancements affect your ability to maintain attention in this scenario?

1 ----- 2 ----- 3 ----- 4 ----- 5 ----- 6 ----- 7 ----- 8

interfered   no effect   helped

12. How did the Display Enhancements affect your ability to maintain situational awareness in this scenario?

1 ----- 2 ----- 3 ----- 4 ----- 5 ----- 6 ----- 7 ----- 8

interfered   no effect   helped

13. How did the Display Enhancements affect your ability to maintain safe traffic flow in this scenario?

1 ----- 2 ----- 3 ----- 4 ----- 5 ----- 6 ----- 7 ----- 8

interfered   no effect   helped

14. How did the Display Enhancements affect your ability to maintain efficient traffic flow in this scenario?

1 ----- 2 ----- 3 ----- 4 ----- 5 ----- 6 ----- 7 ----- 8

interfered   no effect   helped

15. How did the Display Enhancements affect Incident your ability to prioritize control actions in this scenario?

1 ----- 2 ----- 3 ----- 4 ----- 5 ----- 6 ----- 7 ----- 8

interfered   no effect   helped

16. How did the Display Enhancements affect your ability to **detect aircraft** heading to different destinations in this scenario?

1 ----- 2 ----- 3 ----- 4 ----- 5 ----- 6 ----- 7 ----- 8

interfered   no effect   helped

17. How did the Display Enhancements affect your ability to meet restrictions in a timely manner in this scenario?

1 ----- 2 ----- 3 ----- 4 ----- 5 ----- 6 ----- 7 ----- 8

interfered   no effect   helped

18. How did the Display Enhancements affect traffic complexity in this scenario?

1 ----- 2 ----- 3 ----- 4 ----- 5 ----- 6 ----- 7 ----- 8
reduced   no effect   increased

19. If you found that the Display Enhancements had no effect on any of the areas covered in the questions above, please let us know whether you found the enhancement itself to be ineffective or if the scenario was not optimal for using the enhancement.

_____

_____

_____

_____

_____

20. Do you have any other comments about your experiences during this simulation?

_____

_____

_____

_____

_____

_____

Appendix G
Participant Exit Questionnaire

Participant Code _____

In comparison to working without the Display Enhancements…

1. How did the Display Enhancements affect your ability to maintain safe traffic flow?

    1 ----- 2 ----- 3 ----- 4 ----- 5 ----- 6 ----- 7 ----- 8

    interfered   no effect   helped

2. How did the Display Enhancements affect your ability to maintain efficient traffic flow?

    1 ----- 2 ----- 3 ----- 4 ----- 5 ----- 6 ----- 7 ----- 8

    interfered   no effect   helped

3. How did the Display Enhancements affect your ability to maintain attention?

    1 ----- 2 ----- 3 ----- 4 ----- 5 ----- 6 ----- 7 ----- 8

    interfered   no effect   helped

4. How did the Display Enhancements affect your ability to maintain situation awareness?

    1 ----- 2 ----- 3 ----- 4 ----- 5 ----- 6 ----- 7 ----- 8

    interfered   no effect   helped

5. How did the Display Enhancements affect your ability to prioritize control actions?

    1 ----- 2 ----- 3 ----- 4 ----- 5 ----- 6 ----- 7 ----- 8

    interfered   no effect   helped

6. How did the Display Enhancements affect your ability to plan ahead?

    1 ----- 2 ----- 3 ----- 4 ----- 5 ----- 6 ----- 7 ----- 8

    interfered   no effect   helped

7. How did the SUA enhancement affect:

    A: display complexity   1 ----- 2 ----- 3 ----- 4 ----- 5 ----- 6 ----- 7 ----- 8

                                    decreased   no effect   increased

    B: traffic complexity   1 ----- 2 ----- 3 ----- 4 ----- 5 ----- 6 ----- 7 ----- 8

                                    decreased   no effect   increased

    C: cognitive complexity   1 ----- 2 ----- 3 ----- 4 ----- 5 ----- 6 ----- 7 ----- 8

                                    decreased   no effect   increased

8. How did the Overflight enhancement affect:

    A: display complexity   1 ----- 2 ----- 3 ----- 4 ----- 5 ----- 6 ----- 7 ----- 8
                                          decreased   no effect   increased

    B: traffic complexity   1 ----- 2 ----- 3 ----- 4 ----- 5 ----- 6 ----- 7 ----- 8
                                          decreased   no effect   increased

    C: cognitive complexity   1 ----- 2 ----- 3 ----- 4 ----- 5 ----- 6 ----- 7 ----- 8
                                          decreased   no effect   increased

9. How did the Destination Airport enhancement affect:

    A: display complexity   1 ----- 2 ----- 3 ----- 4 ----- 5 ----- 6 ----- 7 ----- 8
                                          decreased   no effect   increased

    B: traffic complexity   1 ----- 2 ----- 3 ----- 4 ----- 5 ----- 6 ----- 7 ----- 8
                                          decreased   no effect   increased

    C: cognitive complexity   1 ----- 2 ----- 3 ----- 4 ----- 5 ----- 6 ----- 7 ----- 8
                                          decreased   no effect   increased

10. When all of the Display Enhancements were presented at the same time, how did the enhancements affect:

    A: display complexity   1 ----- 2 ----- 3 ----- 4 ----- 5 ----- 6 ----- 7 ----- 8
                                          decreased   no effect   increased

    B: traffic complexity   1 ----- 2 ----- 3 ----- 4 ----- 5 ----- 6 ----- 7 ----- 8
                                          decreased   no effect   increased

    C: cognitive complexity   1 ----- 2 ----- 3 ----- 4 ----- 5 ----- 6 ----- 7 ----- 8
                                          decreased   no effect   increased

For the questions below, please circle the number that best describes your experience in this study. Please also provide comments to elaborate on your responses whenever possible.

11. Rate the realism of the simulated pilot responses compared to your field experience.

 1 ----- 2 ----- 3 ----- 4 ----- 5 ----- 6 ----- 7 ----- 8
 unrealistic   moderate   realistic

12. Rate the overall realism of the simulation compared to your field experience.

 1 ----- 2 ----- 3 ----- 4 ----- 5 ----- 6 ----- 7 ----- 8
 unrealistic   moderate   realistic

13. Rate the adequacy of the simulation training.

 1 ----- 2 ----- 3 ----- 4 ----- 5 ----- 6 ----- 7 ----- 8
 inadequate   moderate   adequate

14. What can be done to improve simulation fidelity? What improvements in scenario, traffic, phraseology, and simulation would you suggest? What improvements to equipment would you suggest?

_____

_____

_____

_____

_____

Appendix H

Means (and Standard Deviations) by Enhancement Condition for all Aircraft

Measure	En Route		Arrival		SUA		All Enhancements	
	Enhanced	Control	Enhanced	Control	Enhanced	Control	Enhanced	Control
Total time in sector (s)	58145.71 (3876.30)	59540.57 (8437.42)	52472.14 (4632.97)	52890.00 (5228.40)	51732.57 (5802.40)	49842.43 (8570.98)	54318.75 (5384.93)	55201.88 (6943.74)
Total distance flown (nm)	5549.26 (410.23)	5743.53 (930.25)	4870.26 (460.55)	4910.37 (545.71)	4977.63 (808.93)	4811.71 (717.19)	5043.19 (460.50)	5176.98 (703.52)
Operational errors	0.4 (0.8)	0.9 (0.7)	1.0 (0.6)	0.9 (0.9)	0.9 (0.9)	1.1 (1.5)	2.0 (1.8)	1.9 (1.7)
Altitude changes	63.9 (6.1)	70.4 (5.6)	65.3 (6.2)	67.6 (5.7)	52.0 (4.8)	52.9 (6.1)	67.4 (7.0)	67.5 (7.7)
Heading changes	21.7 (8.6)	23.3 (8.2)	24.6 (6.7)	33.1 (8.6)	58.0 (7.2)	54.6 (9 8)	49.9 (9.0)	56.4 (16.3)
Speed changes	5.3 (3.4)	7.3 (3.6)	12.9 (9.1)	13.7 (5.8)	9.1 (5.0)	5.9 (4.0)	3.8 (2.2)	4.1 (3.6)

Appendix I

Means (and Standard Deviations) by Enhancement Condition for Enhanced Aircraft

Measure	En Route		Arrival		All Enhancements	
	Enhanced	Control	Enhanced	Control	Enhanced	Control
Total time in sector (s)	24108.0 (5188.4)	24508.7 (3272.0)	29648.6 (2422.3)	29973.0 (2484.3)	44337.4 (4677.4)	44978.4 (4932.1)
Total distance flown (nm)	2400.3 (492.3)	2524.0 (451.9)	2432.6 (225.5)	2448.4 (182.5)	3953.5 (394.7)	4050.4 (440.6)
Operational errors	0.0	0.0	0.0	0.0	1.1 (1.1)	1.0 (0.9)
Altitude changes	0.4 (0.5)	1.0 (1.5)	42.7 (2.4)	46.6 (3.6)	46.1 (6.9)	44.3 (8.0)
Heading changes	5.1 (6.0)	5.6 (4.3)	12.6 (4.9)	19.3 (8.4)	27.4 (5.5)	28.9 (8.0)
Speed changes	0.0	0.1 (0.4)	11.9 (7.7)	13.1 (5.6)	3.4 (2.3)	3.8 (3.0)